What people are saying about …

RISE UP & SING

"As a worship leader, Lex leads with great boldness and sensitivity. Her vulnerability and guts to step out in the things of God have always inspired me in my own spiritual walk. This book is an effective and inspiring tool for people learning and cultivating their gifts as leaders of congregational worship."

Tim Hughes, lead worshipper and songwriter

"What can I say? Lex has done an absolutely fantastic job of presenting a very real issue in the church today with a biblical understanding of truthful worship and with a heart to serve people. I'm so very proud of this important accomplishment, and I wholeheartedly pray that this book is a real gift—to both men and women in worship ministry. I am so grateful for what God has stirred in Lex's heart and thankful to see this book now a reality as a product of her fervor and dedication to seeing *you* step into this very holy calling with confidence and peace. I pray each of us would always see that leading others in worship is all about Jesus, and always approach it in that regard. I look forward to hearing some of the great stories that result from the revelation received as you read on."

Darlene Zschech, lead worshipper,
songwriter, and author

"Lex Buckley leads worship with much heart, and this great little book is full of the same. *Rise Up and Sing* is packed with practical and passionate teaching which will equip and encourage women worship leaders everywhere."

Matt Redman, lead worshipper and songwriter

"Thank you, Lex, for writing this book! It's time for us women worshippers to step forward and embrace the mantle of leadership God has called us to—and what an amazing gift of encouragement this book is. Lex has shared so honestly and openly her own challenges and victories (so many of which I can personally relate to!), while giving practical advice and excellent Bible teaching. Take an afternoon out, recline on a comfy sofa with a cup of tea and some chocolate, and read through the chapters of this book. With an open heart, open Bible, a journal, and a pen let the Holy Spirit encourage and teach you, that you may truly become the wonderful woman He has created you to be."

Nikki Fletcher, recording artist, Worship Central

"Lex's book is not just a handy guide to leading worship, but a truly personal journal of the joys and struggles God has led her through to become who she is today: an inspiring and influential worship leader to thousands of young women across the world. Lex shares her honest, practical, and worked-out advice in a way that spans the range of experience: from those who have just started leading worship in a small group to those who are pastoring a team of musicians at their church. Wherever you're at on your journey, there is something in here for you! In a society where the church has only just begun to see women emerge into positions of leadership, I pray that this book would be a catalyst for girls to discover, pursue, and grow in their calling to *rise up and sing!*"

Beth Croft, recording artist, Soul Survivor

"Lex gives us a much-needed resource for the female worship leader in *Rise Up and Sing*. Her passion for worshipping God is clear and her use of Scripture throughout this book brings a solid foundation to her writing. This is a great book for anyone involved in church leadership, male or female."

Kelly Minter, author of
No Other gods, speaker, singer

"*Rise Up And Sing* is a wonderful resource for women wanting to lead worship in today's church. It is refreshing that Lex does not shy away from all topics of leading as a woman, but with grace and wisdom she tackles each of them. Whether a brand-new or seasoned worship leader, this book is an encouragement that women have a place, strength, and uniqueness as worship leaders and that we are not alone in this journey!"

Bekah Wagner, worship leader,
New Life Church and The Desperation Band

RISE UP & SING

**Equipping the Female
Worship Leader**

LEX BUCKLEY

**With contributions from Beth Redman,
Christy Nockels, and Kathryn Scott**

David C Cook®
transforming lives together

RISE UP AND SING
Published by David C. Cook
4050 Lee Vance View
Colorado Springs, CO 80918 U.S.A.

David C. Cook Distribution Canada
55 Woodslee Avenue, Paris, Ontario, Canada N3L 3E5

David C. Cook U.K., Kingsway Communications
Eastbourne, East Sussex BN23 6NT, England

Survivor is an imprint of David C. Cook
Kingsway Communications Ltd
info@survivor.co.uk

David C. Cook and the graphic circle C logo
are registered trademarks of Cook Communications Ministries.

The Web site addresses recommended throughout this book are offered as a
resource to you. These Web sites are not intended in any way to be or imply an
endorsement on the part of David C. Cook, nor do we vouch for their content.

Unless otherwise noted, all Scripture quotations are taken from the *Holy Bible,
New International Version*®. *NIV*®. Copyright © 1973, 1978, 1984 by International
Bible Society. Used by permission of Zondervan. All rights reserved. Scripture
quotations marked MSG are taken from *THE MESSAGE*. Copyright © by Eugene
H. Peterson 1993, 1994, 1995, 1996, 2000, 2001, 2002. Used by permission of
NavPress Publishing Group. Luke 6:45 quote in foreword is taken from the HOLY
BIBLE, TODAY'S NEW INTERNATIONAL VERSION®. Copyright © 2001,
2005 by Biblica®. Used by permission of Biblica®. All rights reserved worldwide.

LCCN 2010923351
ISBN 978-1-4347-0058-2
eISBN 978-1-4347-0218-0

© 2010 Lex Buckley

The Team: Les Moir, Sally Johnson, Richard Herkes, Liza Hoeksma,
Amy Kiechlin, Jack Campbell, and Karen Athen
Cover Design: Sarah Schultz
Cover Photo: iStockphoto

Printed in the United States of America
First Edition 2010

1 2 3 4 5 6 7 8 9 10

042710

To Bella

You are the most beautiful gift. I love you so much and I cannot wait to see all that God is going to do in and through you.

Contents

Foreword

From the moment I first met Lex, I knew she had a great big heart for God. Then I heard her sing—and realized that this great big heart for God was connected to her vocal chords! Jesus said that "out of the overflow of the heart the mouth speaks"—and from hearing Lex sing and from seeing her write songs and lead worship, I could tell that it was simply the overflow of her love for Jesus. That's always the starting point: a heart amazed by the love of God and in awe of who He is. As we begin to lead worship, we build on this all of the practical skills we need in order to write and lead songs of worship—but the foundation will always be a heart devoted to Jesus, one that is filled with wonder, love, and praise.

That sense of love and devotion for God is all over this wonderful book for women worship leaders. Lex speaks passionately and purposefully to instruct and encourage lady lead worshippers everywhere. Perhaps you've been discouraged by the environment you lead in or have always felt a little lacking in confidence in a worship-band setting where most others are male. Maybe you wonder if past hurts disqualify you from leading others before the throne of God in music. Perhaps you've never ventured into songwriting. Lex speaks into so many issues like these to build you up in Christ and to see you raised up as a singer of songs for Him.

One of the wonderful things about this book is the number of practical examples on how to grow in our gifts. Lex welcomes in other leaders to speak into these themes too, such as Christy Nockels and Kathryn Scott. All of these pieces of teaching and encouragement blend together well to give some really helpful suggestions for how to move forward in our leadership skills.

Not only is Lex passionate about Jesus, but she is also passionate about His church. That shines through on every page of this book. I know that those who read it will find themselves equipped to love, lead, and serve their local churches like never before. May you lead the people of God boldly and gently—with both femininity and humility!

I hope you enjoy this book as much as I did.

With much love,
Beth Redman
Cowriter of the songs
"Blessed Be Your Name"
and "Let My Words Be Few"

A word from a pastor

In the first few months of Lex being on staff at our church, I had a conversation with her in my office that led to her leaving in tears. I had no idea exactly what I had said or done, but I knew I had really upset her. This was the beginning of God showing me that leading women was very different from leading men! Since that time God has used Lex to challenge me as a church leader to treat and lead all of my staff members in unique and specific ways that help them grow into the people and leaders God has called them to be.

Lex has been with us now for three years, and even though she is young, she is one of the most gifted and loyal leaders with whom I have ever worked. As well as heading up our worship department with her husband, Paul, Lex also has influence over multiple areas of our church and ministry. She is constantly reminding me of our values and has proved to be a gifted and respected staff member whom I go to for input on the church's most important decisions. However, as gifted as she is, she is someone who does not take herself too seriously—she's definitely not afraid to be real!

From the very beginning of her time here at River City Church, Lex's love and passion for Jesus and her desire to see His church grow and thrive have been so evident. She is passionate about seeing God's people healed and restored, for them to step out and be all that they were created to be, and she wants to do all that she can to encourage and equip female worship leaders. That's why she wrote this book. If you are a woman who feels called to lead worship, this book is for you! You will certainly be inspired and equipped to step out and be the worship leader you were created to be. I highly recommend this book and look forward to seeing the impact it will have on the future generation of female worship leaders.

Antley Fowler
Senior Pastor of River City Church
Jacksonville, Florida

Introduction

I love boys. I always have. I remember having my first crush when I
was three years old on this little boy at my kindergarten who was a
total cutie! It was actually boys that led me to go to my local church
youth group where I became a Christian. I was in seventh grade when
a friend invited me to go to her youth group pool party. I had never
really been to a church event like that before, but when I arrived and
realized that it was filled with gorgeous boys, I was hooked! Now,
fifteen years later, I'm married to an amazing man whom I love to
pieces, and I live my life to follow our Savior, Jesus, with all my heart.

So even though this is a book for women where I look at the joys
and struggles of being a female worship leader, please know that I
think men are fantastic! I don't want women to take over the world.
I am just passionate about seeing women be all that God has created
them to be, and to see men and women using their gifts to work
together for His glory. As a female worship leader, I long to see other
women rise up and lead worship, and I want to do anything I can to
encourage and equip those who feel called to lead. It's this passion
that led me to write this book. I know that, like me, many women

don't have a more experienced female worship leader to invest in them and train them, so I wanted to write the book I wish someone had given me when I started leading. This book includes everything I thought might help you along your journey, from the practical to the spiritual and emotional aspects of being a female worship leader. My hope is that as you read this book, you will be filled with the confidence found only in Christ to step out and be all that He has created you to be for His glory.

A note before we start

I want us to begin this journey by understanding not just *how* we worship but also *why* we worship. We learn in Genesis that from the very beginning God created us for Himself, to enjoy relationship with Him and to bring Him praise and glory. We therefore worship God as our Creator. But we also worship God as our Savior and Redeemer. Our worship is therefore a response to both who He is and what He has done in rescuing us and reconciling us to Himself. First John 4:10 states, "This is love: not that we loved God, but that he loved us and sent his Son as an atoning sacrifice for our sins." John goes on to write, "We love because he first loved us." The implication is that the more we are in touch with God's love and saving grace, the more likely we are to respond in passionate worship, both personally and corporately. At a personal level, our response of worship is something that involves the whole of our lives. Paul says in 1 Corinthians 10:31, "Whether you eat or drink or whatever you do, do it all for the glory of God." Yet at the same time, as much of the rest of this book explores, there also has to be a corporate response.

I don't know what your experience of corporate worship is—if the services at your local church include extended times of worship, or use songs as "hymn sandwiches" to break up the service into manageable chunks, or even use the worship as a warm-up for the sermon. But biblically speaking, worship is not a warm-up for anything: It is the central activity of God's people. The Bible commands us to gather together and worship Him through song: "Sing to the LORD, you saints of his; praise his holy name" (Psalm 30:4); "Sing psalms, hymns and spiritual songs with gratitude in your hearts to God" (Colossians 3:16). The Psalms also encourage us to offer praise with musical instruments: "Praise him with tambourine and dancing, praise him with the strings and flute, praise him with the clash of cymbals" (Psalm 150:4–5).

Through such worship we participate in the worship of heaven. We join the angels (as well as Christians across the world) around the throne of God as we worship and participate here and now in what we will experience fully when Christ returns. So let us worship God with our whole lives and gather together to pour out our love to Him with all our heart, with all our soul, with all our mind, and with all our strength.

1

The call to lead

Do you ever look around you and wonder where all the female worship leaders are? I don't know about you, but I predominantly see men leading worship. In many cases this is because women have not been encouraged to step into any church leadership roles. But amidst this reality is one thing that excites me more than anything: Through all the arguments for and against women in leadership roles, we see in the Bible that God *does* use women to lead His people in worship.

The book of Exodus tells us about the life of Miriam. We don't know too much about Miriam, but we do know she was a prophetess and one of the leaders of Israel alongside her brother Aaron (they both led under the authority of Moses). She was also a worshipper. In Exodus 15:20–21, after God had parted the Red Sea and the Israelites had escaped the Egyptians, it says, "Then Miriam the prophetess, Aaron's sister, took a tambourine in her hand, and all the women followed her, with tambourines and dancing. Miriam sang to them: 'Sing to the LORD, for he is highly exalted. The horse and its rider he has hurled into the sea.'"

The word *sing* in Hebrew used here is *shiru*, which is a masculine, plural command. This means that Miriam is addressing men and women in verse 21. The natural reading of the Hebrew is that Miriam leads a group of women who become her backing vocalists (so to speak) as she leads the whole community in worship. Some might question that she actually *led* them in worship because it says she sang *to* them.

But throughout the Psalms, we see the psalmists write songs like this, encouraging others to worship God (Psalm 30:4; Psalm 33:1–3). The psalmists wrote songs *to* God, *about* God, and *to* the Israelites encouraging them to worship God, just as many worship songs do today.

Miriam's response to what God had done was to worship Him and then encourage the people of Israel to worship Him with her. At the end of the day, a worship leader is a passionate worshipper who through their voice and instrument encourages others to worship God as they seek to worship Him themselves. And this is what Miriam did. She was a worshipper whom God used to lead His people in worship for His glory.

So now that we know that God *does* use women to lead worship, the question is whether He is calling *you* to lead. Here are some general questions you might want to ask yourself to begin the process of finding your answer.

Are you a passionate worshipper?

The most obvious and important question is, do you *love* to worship God? More than anything a worship leader must be a worshipper. Genuine worshippers are people who are just as passionate about pouring out their praise to God when they are on their own as when they are at church. As Mike Pilavachi, leader of Soul Survivor Ministries in the UK, always says, "You can't lead people somewhere you haven't been yourself." Our first passion must always be to worship God, and it's only out of our passion to worship Him that He will call us to lead others.

Do you have the practical skills required to lead worship?

Another important factor is skill. Can you sing in tune? Are you musical? You don't have to have an incredible voice to lead worship, but if you can't sing in tune, leading sung worship might not be your gift. Not everyone who starts out leading worship has a fantastic voice or is an incredible musician (and not all worship leaders lead on an instrument), but if you're called to lead worship, usually those in leadership over you will see your potential, and it will be clear to them that you are someone to invest in.

Have others confirmed that you are called to lead worship?

If you are called to lead worship, usually those around you will be in agreement. But if leading worship is something that you're

passionate about and you have not been encouraged to step out
in it yet, ask your pastor, ask your friends, ask those around you
who will be honest with you. Make sure you aren't just asking your
mother though! Mine thinks I should try out for *Australian Idol,*
and although I am so grateful that she totally believes in me, I know
full well that I am not gifted enough to do well in a competition
like that! You've got to trust that if you are called to lead worship
and it's the right time for you to step out, those around you will
encourage you to do so.

Are you being given opportunities to lead worship?

If you are called to lead worship, opportunities will arise for you to
do so. I never had to try to push doors open myself—God opened
them in His timing. First, I began singing backing vocals at church.
Then I led worship in my small group for a season. Later I began
coleading at church, and after six months of coleading, I finally
began leading on my own. I know it might seem more appeal-
ing to just start leading up front at church straightaway, but the
journey that God took me on totally prepared me for what was
ahead. Leading a band, trying to remember the lyrics, melody, and
chords for the songs, and arranging the band are all pretty tough
sometimes, especially while trying to listen to the Holy Spirit and
follow where He is leading. I would not have been ready to lead on
my own at church if I had been thrown into it without all those
years of worshipping on my own and leading in small groups. So
value every opportunity given to you, because every opportunity
enables you to learn and grow.

You may not be able to fully answer all these questions yet, but if you feel passionate about leading worship, keep worshipping God. Keep growing in the practical aspects of leading worship, and trust that He will give you confirmation and will open the doors for you to lead if that is something He has created you to do.

2

Embracing all that God has created you to be

Being a girl is amazing. It's so much fun! We get to wear makeup and dress up and shop till we drop with the excuse that it's just what girls do. We aren't afraid to cry. I love that God created us to be emotional—to be romantics. The boys may tease us, but God created us to love movies like *The Notebook*! I love that He made us to be openhearted, to stand with each other as sisters through all seasons of life; that He created us to be nurturing, entrusting many of us with bearing the incredible gifts that children are. I love how our Father in heaven pursues us, longing for us to know that we are His daughters, beautiful and valuable to Him and made in His image to reflect Him. And I love that God has created us to be strong warriors used by Him to bring His kingdom to this earth, united in purpose with the wonderful men He has placed in our lives. I love it.

However, those truths are often hard to hear amongst all that the world and the church have told us over the years. Many of us have been made to feel that who we are and what we bring are not as valuable as who men are and what they bring, that the only role we can play remains in the kitchen and the nursery. We have been told to be quiet, seen but not heard. And if we hear these things or have these boundaries placed around us for long enough, we end up believing these lies and don't step into all that God has for us.

Even now in a culture that is more pro-women, I still feel the effects of those lies spoken for so many years. But it's time to grab hold of the truth, because it's the truth that will set us free to be all that God has created us to be!

Equal but not identical

We read in Genesis 1:27 that "God created man in his own image, in the image of God he created him; male and female he created them." So we see in Genesis that men and women have both been created in the image of God to reflect different aspects of His heart and character. This is a wonderful thing, but because of the oppression that women have been under in the past, and in some places still are, there is a danger that in our fight for equality we have almost tried to disregard our differences. Women want the same job opportunities, the same pay, and the same rights as men. We want equality, and that is totally right. However, being equal to men doesn't mean we are identical to them. We weren't created to be! God created us distinctly different from each other. But where we see men stepping out confidently in their masculinity, we often see women, particularly in leadership positions, hiding aspects of their nature that are uniquely feminine in order to feel that they will be accepted as equal to men.

Genesis 2:25 states, "The man and his wife were both naked, and they felt no shame."

God originally created us to have no shame in the way we were made, both male and female, and I don't think that is just referring to the physical. I believe that before the fall, Adam and Eve were completely free to be themselves in front of each other; they weren't ashamed and they weren't insecure. So we really shouldn't be ashamed of our differences—we need to embrace them.

This is not always easy though. Choosing to believe this truth has been a journey for me. When I first started leading worship, I was surrounded by male worship leaders. Initially I felt a freedom to be myself, but after a while I started to notice the differences in the way I led compared to them. A series of doubts and insecurities started creeping into my mind, and I became worried that the way I led worship was not as good as how the men led, that people preferred it when they led, and that the men didn't like the songs I wrote because they were different from the songs they were writing. Over time I allowed the things that were unique to me to fade into the background in order to fit in, and I stopped fully stepping out in the way God had created me to lead. In reality I just wanted to feel accepted, and I was afraid to fully be myself in fear that men would not think who I am and what I brought as a female worship leader were as valuable.

Proverbs 29:25 says that the fear of others "will prove to be a snare, but whoever trusts in the LORD is kept safe." Fear robs us of joy and of the security that comes from being a child of God. He is our Father, our helper, and our defender. If we are looking to other people more than to God for affirmation, then we are basically saying, "Lord, I know that You say I am valuable, but I am actually going to search for my value in what other people think." As worship leaders we must worship God alone and find our affirmation in Him alone. This is something that God is constantly challenging me to do. We need to choose to be confident in who God says we are, especially when the enemy speaks lies to us. Satan's desire for us is to stay hidden, whereas God is calling us to step out and fully embrace all that He has created us to be.

Will the real me please stand up!

Without a doubt, I am an extrovert. I *love* to be with people. I fully realized this a few years ago when my husband, Paul, was away and I spent three days in a row working from home. By the third day I was feeling totally depressed. And then it suddenly dawned on me—I had not seen *anyone* for *three days,* which in my world is a lifetime! Honestly, I have no idea how Paul and I came together; he and I are pretty much opposites. He'd love a few days on his own, especially if it gave him an escape from my constant chatting! We have totally different personalities.

All of us have been created differently—from the way we look to the personalities and gifts God has given us. I love to wear makeup, blow-dry my hair straight, and dress up nicely. But half the time you'll find me in sweatpants and a hoodie with no makeup at all. I am a funny mixture of girly and tomboy. I've often looked around and seen other women who were always dressed up and looking gorgeous and felt insecure because I'm just not like them. However, God has been showing me that I am the way I am because it's how He designed me, and that He wants me to embrace who He's made me to be, choosing to find my security in Him alone.

Over the past couple of years God has been showing me that I lead so much better when I am myself. For example, my church recently held a women's conference, and because I was hosting it and there were loads of people coming from different churches, I felt that I needed to dress up a bit to look respectable. So I straightened my hair and put on some makeup, and instead of my usual Converse Chuck Taylors, I wore some high-heel boots. They are the only pair of boots I own, and I love them. However, I'd recently been having trouble with one of my knees, and during that first evening session, my knee began to really hurt. I had never led the main sessions for a conference like that before, so I was quite nervous anyway, but the pain in my knee was making it even harder for me to feel comfortable and be myself. When I got home that night, I realized that as much as I was trying to fit the role of a sophisticated high-heel wearer … I had to ditch the boots!

The next morning I got up, put on my Chuck Taylors, and made a joke at the beginning of the morning session about how the whole "boots thing" wasn't going to work. I then let everyone else in the room know that they could be free to be themselves, sweatpants and all! Everyone laughed; I relaxed and led that second session much better.

The way God has created me also spills into the way I lead worship. I love to lead out of that place of sensitivity I have as a woman and sing the more intimate songs. However, I also love to totally go for it in worship and shout out God's praise. My voice is a bit husky, so I don't sound like some of the other female worship leaders I know who have such gorgeous, gentle voices. It's just who I am, and God has challenged me to see my differences as a good thing and not to feel insecure because the way I lead and sing is different from the way others lead and sing.

I am also passionate about seeing people healed and set free, and that's why it's something I sing and write about. I've felt silly sometimes and thought that people were probably thinking, *Why doesn't this girl just pick a new theme! Enough about healing already!* But I have to go for it in this short time I have on earth, to be obedient to what I feel God has called me to and with what He's put on my heart. I've got to be myself!

I had a huge revelation about this when I was in church one day. My husband and I are the worship pastors for River City Church in Jacksonville, Florida, where a couple of years ago my pastor, Antley Fowler, was speaking about worship. He said, "There is something only *you* can bring to God in worship. There is a part of His heart that only *you* can touch, because you are His child and you are unique." And that's when it finally hit home. The fact that my Father in heaven loves it when I, Lex, sing to Him and worship Him just blew me away. Knowing that He valued what I brought to Him changed everything for me. It made all the fears and insecurities I had about what everyone else might think fade away. Now, if ever those thoughts of insecurity start creeping back into my mind, I instantly remember that truth, and I feel safe because I know that the King loves me and delights in me.

There are some amazing female worship leaders and singers out there, and it could be easy to look at the way they sing or lead and, in our admiration for them, try to be like them. Yet we have all been created differently, and God will be able to use us more effectively if we are ourselves. Your church doesn't need another version of someone else. Your church needs *you* and all that *you* bring as you lead them! What you bring to worship no one else can bring. Your voice, your heart, and your skill bless God in a way that no one else can, because you are unique and He created you for Himself. He longs for you to worship Him, just the way you are.

Pursue healing

All of us come into relationship with God and with each other carrying wounds or past hurts. It may be from an experience at school, from a broken heart, or from a broken home. Somewhere along the way we hit bumps in the road, and we experienced pain, loss, and injustice. These wounds can cause our identities to be shaken, leaving us insecure and carrying the pain that Christ came to free us from. It's our brokenness that can make it really hard for us to be ourselves. But leading worship out of a place of honesty is so important. We can't pretend to be something that we're not, or to be at a place we aren't. I am in no way saying that we should share our deepest fears and past hurts when we lead— of course not! When we lead worship, the last thing we want to do is draw attention to ourselves. But I have found that I lead so much better when I am openhearted and vulnerable before God. Being real with God and one another as we lead enables us to lead freely, and it frees those in the congregation to be real before God too. The masks are taken off, and we are able to engage with God more intimately.

However, so often we want to save face, and we want everyone to think we are totally sorted out. Living in Florida, part of the Bible Belt of the United States, it seems that people have been trained to be so incredibly polite, which is amazing; but often they've also been told that you are supposed to present a perfect picture of your life to those around you. Many of the people at my church here in Florida came from churches that expected them to put on their Sunday best for church so that they looked presentable and to come with a smile on their faces even if they were going through a really difficult time. It is definitely biblical to praise God and thank Him and rejoice in Him in seasons that bring us trials and suffering, but God doesn't want us to pretend with Him. He wants us to worship Him in Spirit and truth—to be led by His Spirit and to be honest with Him. This means not keeping any part of our lives shut away from Him. When we are totally open with God and allow Him to enter every area of our lives—our pasts, present, and hopes for the future—He will often bring our wounds to the surface so He can heal us.

Emotional healing is something I've been pursuing for years. I have the most amazing family, and looking back, everyone really did their best to cope with all that came our way with divorce, remarriage, and blending families. But when I was a child, it wasn't always easy to understand it all, and it did take quite a few years for my family to adjust to life with each other. With these things came baggage. I feel very blessed because I have gained an amazing stepdad and both half and stepsiblings, but it did take a bit of time to work through the issues that come up when you have a bunch of people suddenly thrown together. However, it was not just my family situation that caused me to have some issues. I had my heart broken and didn't make the best decisions as a teenager, and I carried baggage from those things too.

So when I moved to the UK to do a discipleship course called SoulTime with Soul Survivor Ministries at the age of nineteen, I came bringing baggage from my past. I knew I needed to work through some of these things, so I asked if there was anyone I could meet with to chat and pray with, and I got introduced to an amazing woman of God named Jeannie. Jeannie and I met on and off for years. Nothing was forced, but when God would bring something up, I just met with her a couple of times, and she would pray for me and would teach me how to bring these things to God myself for healing and freedom. God did so much over these years, and it was often in times of worship at church that I would just cry and give my pain to God. I found healing as I worshipped Him.

Although people around me might have thought it was strange that sometimes I cried during worship, I didn't let the fear of what other people might think shut me down. I remained open to God. It's definitely better to let that pain out than keep it in, because it doesn't go away. It just sits there, seeping into our lives and affecting our thoughts, decisions, and actions.

So pursue inner healing! Deal with your stuff. Bring it to God. You can't do it by yourself. Only Jesus can heal us and free us from these things. God will always use us in our weakness, so I am not saying that you need to have everything together before you step into leadership. It's never going to happen! In fact, it is in our weakness that we rely on God's strength and that His power can be released. As He said in 2 Corinthians 12, "My grace is sufficient for you, for my power is made perfect in weakness." However, God does not desire us to remain bound—He wants us to be free from the things that have held us back.

It is amazing to see God at work in the lives of others, healing them and freeing them so that they can worship Him. A friend shared an example of this with me recently. A girl named Sarah started coming to her church a couple of years ago. She had musical training and could sing, and from the very beginning she had expressed her desire to lead worship. Sarah told my friend about her wounds from her previous church. She shared her hurt and frustration at the leaders of her old church, who knew her desire to lead worship but, during the eight years she sang in the choir, had never given her the opportunity to lead. Because of this she felt totally discouraged, crushed, and insecure and felt a great need to prove herself.

My friend saw the gift this girl had and involved her in the worship team as a backing vocalist and keyboard player. However, she did not put her in a position of leadership, much to Sarah's disappointment. My friend could see that Sarah had to receive healing from these wounds before she could lead worship at church.

Over the past two years, God has done amazing work in Sarah's life. I learned recently that there has been a breakthrough in Sarah's life and that God has really been healing her and dealing with those issues. She no longer feels that she needs to prove herself, and she feels accepted and valued as part of the worship team, which she never felt at her previous church. Sarah is still on that journey of healing, but God has brought her a long way, teaching her that her worth is found in Him and not in any role she might play at church. Sarah recognizes the changes God has made in her and is now grateful that my friend did not put her in a leadership position earlier.

God loves you too much to let you stay bound by things of the past. He wants you to be free so that you can be all He has created you to be. So ask Him if there is anything He wants you to bring before Him, and just follow His leading through the process of healing. If you don't know where to start, a great resource that may help you is a book called *Let the Healing Begin* by Jeannie Morgan (the woman who helped me work through my issues).

Sometimes we need the help others can bring, whether it's someone to chat with or someone to pray with. Don't feel afraid or embarrassed to seek help, whether it's meeting up with a counselor or getting someone to pray through it all with you. Go for it, girls—get healed up!

3

The heart of a worship leader

Today's world is obsessed with celebrities. Countless TV shows, magazines, and Web sites are dedicated to giving us all the latest information about the lives of the rich and famous. Reality TV is getting more and more popular, giving the opportunity for ordinary people to get their fifteen minutes of fame. When you think about it, it's complete madness!

Sadly, it seems the ways of the world have found their way into worship. Many of us have been sucked into the lie that we become more valuable if we are well known and adored by other people. For some, the goal has become having songs sung around the world, leading worship at big events, receiving affirmation and praise from other people, and even making money. Don't get me wrong—there are many songs that have been used to bless the worldwide church. And those of us who are leading worship week in and week out at our local churches have been so refreshed when we have attended worship events and have been led by others. It has given us much-needed space to worship without any responsibility and to be filled up again. But if we begin to pursue writing the next worship "hit" or being up onstage in front of thousands, our eyes are fixed on the wrong things. God opens those doors for some, but our desire should be to serve our local churches and lead those people in His praise. Our eyes need to be fixed on Jesus, and Jesus alone.

It's all about relationship

It can be easy for us to become preoccupied with the little things in our lives and to get busy doing so much that we neglect our relationship with Jesus. In Luke 10, we find Jesus at the home of a woman named Martha. Verses 39–42 reveal that while her sister Mary was sitting at Jesus' feet and listening to Him, Martha was "distracted by all the preparations that had to be made." Feeling annoyed that Mary wasn't helping her, she went to Jesus and asked, "Lord, don't you care that my sister has left me to do the work by myself? Tell her to help me!" But Jesus answered, "Martha, Martha, ... you are worried and upset about many things, but only one thing is needed. Mary has chosen what is better, and it will not be taken away from her." Jesus knew what was better because He chose intimacy with the Father above all else. We read in Mark 1:35 that "very early in the morning, while it was still dark, Jesus got up, left the house and went off to a solitary place, where he prayed," and it was out of His relationship with His Father that He did everything. As my pastor, Antley, says, "There is no shortcut to intimacy; there's no substitute for spending time with Him." We need to be spending time in His presence (Psalm 23).

Like many other worship leaders, before I ever had an opportunity to lead anyone in worship, I used to be in my room all the time worshipping God. Even though I look back and see that God was preparing me to lead, at the time the thought never entered my mind. Leading worship wasn't my goal. I was working as a secretary, and because I am a creative person, the fact that I had to sit at a desk all day kind of drained the life out of me. However, I remember taking the long bus ride home every day and just being desperate to spend time with God and worship Him. When I would arrive home, I would rush to my room, grab my guitar, and just start worshipping the Lord. Although my guitar playing wasn't that great at the time, my personal worship time with God was so special to me, and it's where my love for the Lord and worshipping Him really began to grow.

It's not about us

Because the world around us is cheering us on to make life all about us and what we can achieve, pride is a trait that is often encouraged. So many of the people we see in the public eye are out to promote themselves. Many of them even surround themselves with a team of people paid to make them famous and tell them how fantastic they are!

But the world's ways are not God's ways, and the Bible warns us against being prideful. Proverbs 16:18 says, "Pride goes before destruction, a haughty [arrogant] spirit before a fall," and Proverbs 11:2 states, "When pride comes, then comes disgrace, but with humility comes wisdom." These verses may sound harsh, but their point is a huge wake-up call, isn't it? All of us are going to struggle with pride at times. It's something that will try to creep into our lives. So we need to be actively pursuing humility. John the Baptist said, "He must become greater; I must become less" (John 3:30). This has to be our goal.

In order to quickly recognize pride in our hearts, we need to be self-aware and pay attention to the way we treat people and to the ways we respond when they encourage us and when they criticize us. We need to surround ourselves with people who we are accountable to, who will challenge us, who will be honest with us; and like David in Psalm 139:23–24, we need to come before God and say:

> Search me, O God, and know my heart;
> test me and know my anxious thoughts.
>
> See if there is any offensive way in me,
> and lead me in the way everlasting.

This can be painful at times because God will often reveal where we are struggling with pride, but it opens up the door for us to be humbled. Leading people in worship is a wonderful privilege, and our hearts must be seeking to lift Jesus up and make *Him* known, not to make our names known. God can use us to do amazing things if we humble ourselves and rely on His strength and His Spirit!

Tip: Find a couple of people in your life whom you can regularly ask whether they see anything in you that needs to change. Give them freedom to be honest with you and

to challenge you. Being challenged is not something that
any of us look forward to. It's painful to see where we have
hurt someone or had a bad attitude, but if we don't know,
we will never change!

It's about having integrity

We all fall short. We all make mistakes. There are going to be times
when we do or say things that hurt others or hurt ourselves. And as
leaders, it's really important that we have integrity. Having integrity
is not being perfect; it's just being honest, being known, and not
presenting ourselves on the outside in a way that is inconsistent with
what's on the inside. Personally, I always want to know that the leaders of my church know who they have up front leading worship. I
want them to know me, the good and the bad, so that if they know
my struggles and continue to trust me to lead the church in worship,
I can walk in freedom and confidence to do so. I am not saying that
every single time you have a bad attitude you need to confess to the
whole leadership of your church. Sometimes we just need to bring
these things to God or share with a good friend privately. We need
to make sure that we are known and respond with a teachable heart
when people challenge us. The leaders of our churches are there to
support and cover us, and they can do this best when they know us!

4

How are *you* going to lead?

God calls us in our uniqueness to lead worship in a way that reflects how He has created us. Strength and beauty reside in the differences between ourselves and others. You may already play an instrument, so choosing to lead on that instrument may be a natural choice for you. However, there are a variety of ways to lead, most commonly on guitar, keys, or with no instrument at all. There's no right or wrong choice. They are all great; you just have to go with whatever works for you. You'll find benefits and challenges in any form of leading, so in order to help you along your journey of figuring out how you are going to lead, let's have a look at the options.

Leading on guitar

Leading worship on acoustic guitar was a natural choice for me. I began playing when I was about sixteen years old, and although I knew how to play piano a bit, I was just drawn more to the guitar when it came to choosing a main instrument to lead on.

Freedom

There are some great benefits of playing guitar, and one of them is that you have a lot of freedom to move around. This makes communicating with the band easier, which is a huge help when leading worship. You have the freedom to turn around and communicate directly with any of the musicians, and you can use your legs, and at times your hands, to signal to the rest of the band where you are heading next—if you want to repeat a chorus or end the song for example. Here are some of the signals I use to communicate with the band:

- When I want to repeat a chorus, I bend my knee and lift my right or left leg up behind me.

- When I want to end a song, I turn to the drummer and tilt my guitar up slightly.

- If I want only a certain instrument to play, I turn and point to that musician. This signals that particular person to keep playing and the rest of the band to drop out.

- If I want to build a section, I stomp my foot and start building with my guitar.

- If I want to keep the song "down," I hold an arm out behind me, with my palm facing down.

- I also use vocal cues, such as saying the first few words of the next section before I begin singing it. This lets the band and the person operating the lyric projection know what's coming next, especially if I want to go back into a verse we've already sung.

As well as the freedom to communicate easily with the band, when leading on guitar, you have the freedom to change up the set without having to rely on any of the other musicians. As we know and believe, God is alive and moving today! So when we come to lead worship, although we plan as best as we can, there may be moments during times of worship when you feel Him leading you in a different direction than you had practiced. At these moments, playing guitar is fantastic! There have been times when I will signal to the drummer not to click into the next song and will start a completely different song. I'll let the band know what key it's in, and they will then join me as best as they can. At other times, we may have planned to do a song "up," and then I sense that we need to leave some space and start the next song gently. So again, I signal to the drummer and begin the song myself. It's so exciting to know that God is speaking in those moments, so I do the best I can to follow His lead, even if the song doesn't sound as rehearsed. You may not have the freedom to change things up at your church, but for those of us who do, playing the guitar is a great advantage.

Easy to transport

Guitars are relatively lightweight and manageable—you can lift
them on your own, and they fit easily into almost any car. Being so
transportable also makes them ideal when leading worship in small
groups.

The beloved capo

When I started playing guitar, I soon came across the capo, and it
became my new best friend. Some guitarists claim that using a capo
is cheating, but I disagree. I think the capo is a genius invention! It
enables you to change keys easily and to move around the neck less,
which I've found so helpful, especially when trying to remember
the chords and lyrics to songs. It simply makes playing guitar easier,
and that can only be a good thing! Another benefit of using a capo
is that it creates a different sound from a guitarist playing without
one. So the sound can work really well when you have two guitarists playing together, one using a capo and one not.

However, with all of its benefits, leading on guitar does present
some challenges.

Tuning

Guitars need tuning, which is a straightforward task if you are
tuning your guitar while setting up for band practice or before
the service has started. However, even though your guitar may be
perfectly in tune at the beginning of the set, often it de-tunes at
some point during a time of worship. I have had very embarrassing

moments when I've started a song on my own mid-set and my guitar was completely out of tune. I can see the look on people's faces—they know something just doesn't sound right. But I've already started the song so I just have to continue playing and wait for that moment when the band comes in and covers up, at least in part, the horrible sound I am producing. This means tuning your guitar mid-set. In these moments I stop playing and singing, and usually ask another musician to play (to avoid an awkward silence while everyone hears me tuning) and use my stage tuner to tune my guitar for the next song. It's not a difficult task; it's just one challenge you are likely to come across when leading on guitar.

Breaking strings

So you're in the middle of a worship set, and you're singing and playing your heart out, leading the congregation in celebration—and suddenly you hear a *doink* or feel something sting your arm. You look down and see that you've broken a string. It's one of those things that just happens! Changing strings takes time—it's not something you can do in the middle of a set. In order to be prepared for this, as guitarists we need to own or borrow a second guitar to have onstage with us so we can swap them if we break a string.

Guitars are delicate instruments

Unlike the keyboard, acoustic guitars are quite delicate instruments because they are made out of wood, so you have to be careful with them. If you are careless, you can dent them or even break the neck, and this may mean trashing it and having to buy a new one. It's both sad and expensive to break a guitar.

The intimate moments

One of the things I have learned from leading on guitar and observing others is that you have to be able to play quite skillfully to sound good during the intimate moments in worship. You need a delicate touch, and you have to play picking patterns correctly. I have to say that I have many memories of trying to play in those moments and not creating music that was pleasing to the ear! Even though I have been playing guitar for a lot longer than piano, I still find it easier to play keys in a way that reflects the beauty of intimacy in those moments. For me, playing guitar at those times just takes more concentration and lots more practice.

I have found leading on guitar not only fun but also very beneficial. So if it's guitar that you are naturally drawn to lead on, I fully encourage you to go for it! Your fingers may throb with pain after a long practice session, and you may occasionally break a string, but it's a great instrument to lead on and allows you to lead the congregation with great freedom.

Kathryn Scott is now going to share from her experience in leading worship on keys. Kathryn has been leading worship since 1997. Mentored by Brian Doerksen (who wrote classic songs like "Faithful One" and "Come, Now Is the Time to Worship"), she wrote and recorded the song "Hungry" for Vineyard Music in 1999. Since then she has recorded two solo albums with Integrity, including the songs "At the Foot of the Cross (Ashes to Beauty)," "You're Good Lord," "Search Me, Know Me," and "I Belong." Kathryn lives with her husband, Alan, and their two little girls in Northern Ireland, where they pastor the Causeway Coast Vineyard together.

Leading on keys
KATHRYN SCOTT

Sometimes the road the Lord leads us down is the one we least expect, and yet it ends up being the most rewarding! I love that He knows how we are wired and exactly how we'll find our fit in the most wonderful ways—even when we are totally unaware of it to begin with.

I have always been musical. I grew up in a strong Christian home where music was a big feature. At the age of sixteen, I started to play piano and sing backing vocals while other people led worship at church. When I was at college, I tried to lead worship, but I didn't feel confident in it at all—I much preferred playing for someone else and just occasionally leading a song. However, in 1997, I met worship leader Brian Doerksen, and my journey into worship leading really began. (Prior to meeting and being trained by Brian, I had led full sets of worship only three times on my own.)

Brian asked about ten of us to be a part of his band while he was leading worship at different conferences in the UK, and every six weeks or so over a two-year period, we would be Brian's band. I learned more than I can tell you simply from watching up close how Brian led. After a while, he asked me to lead a song for him in one of his sets, and then a few songs, and then he played for me while I led. He would give constructive feedback and wonderful encouragement, and eventually I learned how to lead worship too. I am eternally grateful for his friendship and for the input he gave me.

The benefits and challenges of leading on keys

When leading on keys, you can flow between songs incredibly easily. It's a wonderful instrument to lead with. When it gets to those intimate moments, it's so easy to be gentle and yet melodic. We are able to lead with our instrument as well as our voices in a way that guitarists often find a little more difficult to do.

By contrast, one of the challenges has to be the lack of movement. We can't move around the stage, and if we're sitting, we can't turn our whole body to talk to the band. But again, we get to communicate in different ways. It forces us to discover new ways of communicating, and I love the creativity and freedom that brings.

Communicating with the band when leading on keys

When we lead worship, we are creating a safe place where people can engage with God intimately and honestly. To do that, we need to make sure we are all reading off the same page as a band—one in heart and one in skill.

At my church we spend two hours practicing as a band during the week before we lead on a Sunday (and an extra hour on Sunday

morning, too). We want to make sure we've worked on arrangements well, using ones that will sound fresh and full with the band
that we've got. For example, we don't have an electric guitarist at
the moment, so we have to come up with creative ways to use bass,
Hammond, riffs on the piano, and funky drum patterns, etc.

As we practice, we write down everything we are doing on our
chord charts. That way, when we come back to it on Sunday, we'll be
able to remember the ideas we had.

But when we are actually in the middle of the set, a number of
other factors come into play, things we simply can't practice. There
is the dynamic of the congregation and the things that the Lord is
doing while His people engage with Him. We need to be able to do
unscripted things, and for those moments to sound as though we
rehearsed them thoroughly, we need to communicate!

If I want the song to go big at the end of a chorus and go back
into a chorus where we haven't planned one, I will bounce up and
down just where I'm standing. The drummer sees me, and he takes it
back up. If we get to the end of a chorus and we had planned to go
big but I feel like it needs to come down, I stand very still. The drummer then knows that this is the sign for us to gently bring it down.
Before we lead, I always tell the guys that if I start to sing something
spontaneous, we'll be using the chords for the intro during that part;
and if I start to bounce, it's time to bring it up; or if I stand really still,
we'll just keep it quiet.

Our communication isn't just with our band but with the people
we are leading. People don't feel all that safe to sing with gusto, for
example, if they're not entirely sure where you are going next. So
if we've been singing a bridge or are coming out of a spontaneous

moment, I'll sing or shout out the words of the next part. Not only does everyone know what to sing next, but the band gets to know for sure what is coming too.

Some tips for those who lead worship on keys

When you play keys in a guitar world, you need to learn to play with a lot of rhythm. You're forced to develop a style that "sounds right" in the context of songs that weren't written with piano in mind. I love that! It means as pianists we get to be completely unique. We have to work harder at getting that sound, but it's so worth it!

I have always felt a little insecure about the way I play. You may feel the same, but when you're leading, you just need enough confidence not to ruin the set. The playing part has to be good enough to blend well with the band (so we do need to be as good as we can), but it doesn't need to be a virtuoso performance.

I encourage you to really listen to how the mix of instruments sounds and the way your playing blends in with everyone else's. If it sounds great—wonderful! If it sounds too busy, don't be afraid to play less—the band will carry it.

Working with the keyboard player in your band

I am a straight pianist. I rely on others to play synth and pads for me—so if you are doing just that in a band, I want to say thank you for what you bring. I know that playing pads isn't very exciting and that it can feel like all you're doing is just holding a note here or adding a chord there, but what it adds to the overall sound of the arrangement can be breathtaking. Never be tempted to think that "unbusy" is unimportant. It simply isn't true!

Things don't always go as planned!

I think the single most embarrassing moment for me was when I was leading worship a couple of years ago, and I don't think I've quite recovered from it yet! We were moving from one song to another, but they were in different keys. The plan was that I would transpose in my head (which I had done successfully loads of times before) and then just start singing in the new key. Risky but effective—usually. So I started to sing …

Have you ever had that feeling when you realize all is not well but you are in front of a lot of people and there is no turning back? That was the feeling. It was an almost out-of-body experience as I heard myself singing in a completely different key from the band, who were now playing with me. I can honestly say the vocal acrobatics that ensued have scarred me slightly as a person ever since. In fact, I haven't tried it again!

Leading worship is one of the most exciting, challenging, heart-thumpingly enjoyable things! We are so privileged to be able to lead others right into the presence of the King—and of course, where the King is, the kingdom is as well. It's incredible to me that people can become healed and set free, changed and challenged, comforted and made whole simply because they are in His presence. And as worship leaders we have a part to play in facilitating the "meeting place"—the point of connection between us and God.

I want to encourage you to pursue the Father with your whole heart. Allow Him to shape you; give yourself to becoming all that you were created to be—embracing completely the dream that the Father Himself dreamed over you while you were still being knit together in the womb. Learn to hear the whisper of heaven as God beckons you further and further into relationship with Him. He'll speak to you for others too, but it starts with us knowing at our core that we are treasured daughters. And then, daughters, "sing, sing your hearts out to God! Let every detail in your lives—words, actions, whatever—be done in the name of the Master, Jesus, thanking God the Father every step of the way" (Colossians 3:16–17 MSG).

Christy Nockels is now going to share from her experience in leading worship without an instrument. Christy is a worship leader and singer-songwriter who makes her home in Atlanta, Georgia, with her husband, Nathan, and their three children. Christy and Nathan, formerly known as the band Watermark, have toured nationwide for the past twelve years and currently lead worship for Passion Conferences and Passion City Church. Christy's heart through leading and writing is to help people communicate intimately with the living God and to leave a legacy of proclaiming Jesus' fame to this generation.

Leading without an instrument
CHRISTY NOCKELS

I remember when I first heard the words "becoming a *lead worshipper*." I was twenty-two years old, listening to Louie Giglio, founder of Passion Conferences, as he shared his heart to a roomful of collegiate worship leaders. My husband and I were already leading at our local church at the time, but we certainly were not experienced by any means. I look back on that first Passion Conference as a moment when I could finally put words to what I had felt stirring in me for so long. I longed to be more than just a "song leader," but to begin the journey of becoming a true worshipper of God. I wanted to worship, not just with my song, but also with my life! When Louie simply flipped those two words around for us that day, it was revolutionary for me. To be a lead worshipper was the concept that God used to completely reframe my thought process about leading worship. It's amazing how you can sense God doing something in you, but He often uses someone else to help articulate and define that stirring and calling.

I grew up in a very musical family. My dad was a pastor, but he was a worship leader before he became a teaching pastor. My mother has had a private piano studio my whole life and still cranks out lessons every week. I spent countless hours singing with my parents, learning to harmonize as a child and hold the melody while they sang parts. It was such an amazing training ground for loving music and the Word of God. However, with all of that musicality running through my family, I never mastered an instrument. There's a part of me that still gets frustrated at that thought. Believe me, I've had my share of days kicking myself that I didn't practice the piano more or really take the time to perfect the guitar after I spent money on lessons. I can get around on both instruments enough to write songs, but I wouldn't choose to lead with them unless it was absolutely necessary.

I used to worry about it a lot, until one day the Lord let me see things in a different light. I started to realize that if I truly desired to play an instrument, I would work at it every day in order to have that option. I've gone through seasons of picking up the guitar or playing the piano again, but it was mostly because I felt like it was a "must" in order to lead and not necessarily because I desired it. There came a time when I felt like God specifically showed me some things about how He has wired me to do what I do. Leading without an instrument, I have the unique opportunity to visually lead others in a posture of freedom. In other words, there's something to be said about having both hands free in complete surrender. I truly believe that the part of the ministry I'm honored to carry is to lead others, body and spirit, in such a way that they too might feel the freedom to fully engage with God.

Leading primarily without an instrument is certainly not for everyone; I have friends who feel their world onstage is turned upside down if they don't have their guitars strapped to them. I think that's simply God's way: For some there's much more freedom to steer things musically with an instrument. I love how God has gifted us all uniquely. Don't get me wrong, I might periodically be found behind the piano, leading in a small setting. I'm certainly not saying there's only one way I feel that I can function as a leader. I simply believe that God wired me to lead hands-free most of the time for really good reasons.

Working with others

Another very gratifying aspect of leading the way I do is that I have to maintain a healthy dependence on others. By not using an instrument, I need to wait on others and connect with them musically and spiritually. When I have led for various women's events, I have often taken a young woman to play guitar and sing with me. I believe that God orchestrated it this way so I would continually need to invite others into my world and my leadership.

I have led worship side by side with my husband for the past fifteen years. To have Nathan leading onstage with me is a constant picture to me of the covering I have in him spiritually, as well as musically. Because I can't steer my band musically with an instrument, I rely on Nathan to direct the musicians as he plays. I'm so blessed that he knows me personally and that he has also taken the time to get to know me musically as a worship leader. It seems that God often sets limitations around our gifts so that we lean on each other and let another person shine where we don't. Nathan shines in song arrangements, communicating with the band, and approaching everything we do with excellence and a full heart. He uses a talkback mic that goes directly into the band's ear monitors. I realize not everyone uses ear monitors, but even in the early years of using stage monitors, Nathan had special signals for the band. Nathan reads my signals and then communicates them to the other musicians. These are some of the signals that have worked well for us:

- If I'm feeling like a section should build, I will stomp my right foot.

- If we had planned to build in a section but I'm now feeling that we need to take it down completely, I simply hold out my right hand low to my side with my palm facing down.

- If I'd like to repeat a section, I make circles with my pointer finger low at my side.

- When I'd like to end the song at any point, I will make a fist, low to my side, which lets Nathan know that I'd like him to gracefully end the song how he sees fit.

Now I realize that I have the advantage of being married to a very talented guy, but any musician in your band who has a great grasp on the arrangements of the songs can be your bandleader. You can work out some signals that he or she can read, and then this person can take care of getting the band where you need to go. It could be your drummer, your keyboard player, or your guitarist—anyone you work well with and trust.

I love collaborating and connecting with other musicians and leaders. I love being a small part of something bigger. In fact, the more I grow and learn, the more I see that the best things I've done in ministry, both leading worship and writing songs, have been when I've partnered with others. I always sense a powerful anointing when there are two or more of us leading together. I've actually arrived at the place where I prefer it over leading alone. I love learning from others.

I've had some amazing teachers through the years. Nathan and I first led with our friend Charlie Hall over fifteen years ago. Charlie has an amazing ability to exhort the people of God. He shows a very raw way of presenting the great exchange that happens when we worship our Creator … it's beauty for ashes, and it was coleading with Charlie that taught me how to "teach" worship. Leading with Chris Tomlin has taught me to approach God with energy and joy when leading His people—to simply go for it! Tim Hughes has taught me to lead with great passion, both spiritually and melodically; while in Matt Redman a wonderful pastoral gift shines when he leads. I've led worship with most of these guys since before so many people knew their songs and their names. They were, and still are, faithfully serving wherever God has placed them. You too have these kinds of people around you right now—leaders whom you can serve and learn from.

I remember approaching the opportunity to colead with some trepidation. However, after having coled with these guys over the years, I've realized that they do not expect anything of me other than what God has called me to do! They are not looking for the power singer of the universe; they are looking for a fellow worship leader who is walking in the gifts that God has ordained for her—one who is looking to God, not people, for her validation and stamp of approval. One who is relying fully on the Spirit of God to lead her in reverence, humility, and gentleness.

One of my prayers as a coleader is that the Spirit of God would lead me in appropriateness (I know it sounds like it's not a real word, but it is!), so that all eyes would be fixed on Jesus. I have a philosophy, especially when leading with others, that goes like this: *Just because you can, doesn't mean you should!* You may be able to sing loud or high or nail vocal "licks" and "runs," but that doesn't mean it's appropriate for where you are and what you're doing. I'm not saying that you should never step out and be featured; I'm just saying we should choose those moments wisely. One of the most important things you can learn as a coleader is when not to sing! Ask the Spirit of God to guide you in that every time you lead. Ask Him to lead you appropriately, that you might lead strongly and not in an overbearing display of yourself.

I'm currently working more on being "ready" as a coleader—being present in the moment enough to step in should they need me to. There have been moments onstage when the other worship leader will look at me to take a verse, and I look back with a face of panic that says, "I'm going to punch you later!" It seems that always happens when we are in a superhigh key or when I don't know all words to the verses! I've had leaders look at me for help with words or to cover for them when their voices are going. Whatever it is, I'm learning to be ready. I'm currently challenged by this and pray that God will give me great wisdom and discernment in how to better serve the leaders around me.

This is just my story and what works best in my life as a leader. I believe that God places desires within each of us to carry out unique leadership in different places of the church. *Lead worshipping* is intricate and complex—all the way down to the instrument we do or do not play. Ephesians 2:10 says, "We are God's workmanship, created in Christ Jesus to do good works, which God prepared in advance for us to do." We each display something specific and unique, equipped in advance to show the unsurpassable greatness of our God.

Coleading

Kathryn, Christy, and I have been writing about the different ways we lead worship, and as you will have noticed, the journey that God has led each of us on has involved coleading worship. Leading worship is definitely not confined to something that we should always do on our own—leading with other worship leaders has many benefits. So to close this chapter, I want to share a few things I've learned over the years that may help make the experience of coleading a successful one for you.

After gaining experience leading in small groups, often the next step is to colead with a more experienced worship leader at church. It allows you to step out, to grow, and to familiarize yourself with leading a band without being thrown into the deep end on your own straightaway. It also helps the church to get to know you by putting you with a familiar worship leader. I found this so helpful when I was starting out. But coleading is not only great for when you're learning to lead; it's also a lot of fun no matter where you are on the journey of leading worship. It's great to mix different styles, to have men and women leading together, or to have multiple worship leaders leading together. For those who are at churches where one worship leader predominantly leads worship during services, coleading is often refreshing for the worship leaders and for the church; and it helps to shift the focus off one person.

Colead with someone you're comfortable with

Leading worship is such a vulnerable experience. Whether you are learning to lead, leading with one of your peers, or training another worship leader, it's ideal to lead with people you know well or at least have spent some time with. It's just hard to communicate well about anything if you're not comfortable with someone. When you are coleading, communication is particularly important because you need to communicate not only with the band but also with each other so you aren't trying to take the congregation in two different directions. If possible, lead with people who you know are "for" you and you feel comfortable with. It makes things so much easier!

Set aside time to prepare together

I have been in coleading situations where, although we had prepared individually beforehand, we met for only five minutes before band practice to work out our final set list. At those times, band practice was all over the place, and I'm not sure if any of us in the band felt very confident in what we were doing. So over the years I have learned that it's really important to take time beforehand to work out the set list and make sure the band's collective vision for that time of worship is united.

Working out band arrangements is equally important. My husband, Paul, and I often colead, and we have found that meeting together to work out the set list and band arrangements before band practice is crucial. There were a couple of times when we first coled together that we didn't prepare the arrangements in advance; and when it came time for band practice, we realized that we had very different ideas of where the songs should go musically. We decided from then on that we would take more time before band practice to work out the set list *and* arrangements together. It meant that we could talk through our questions or disagreements privately and come to band practice ready to lead well together. It has made such a difference!

Training others

As someone who was trained to lead with others, I know how important it is to feel supported and believed in by the more experienced worship leader. So when training other worship leaders, make sure you are encouraging them to go for it and letting them know that you believe in them. Let them communicate to the band when practicing the songs they are going to lead, even though you may do a better job of it. It's the only way they will grow in confidence and become familiar with their new leadership role. If they feel supported by you, knowing that you believe in them and that it's okay to make mistakes, they will grow and thrive in their new role.

5

How to prepare for and
lead a band practice

When I first started leading worship, I really had no idea what I was doing. I loved the Lord, I loved to worship Him, and I had been singing backing vocals on my church worship team for a couple of years, so I had many opportunities to observe other worship leaders. However, when it came time for me to prepare for and lead band practice, I definitely fumbled my way through it.

In order to make things a bit easier if you are just starting out, I thought it would be helpful to give a step-by-step guide to preparing to lead worship by telling you some things I've learned along the way. I also want to look at some of the obstacles you may come across as a female worship leader and share with you some of the practices I've used to help me get through them.

Step 1: Seek Him

The first step to preparing to lead a band practice is to seek the heart of God for that time of worship. Worship is often described as a journey, and we see this throughout the Psalms. Psalm 100:4 says to "enter his gates with thanksgiving and his courts with praise; give thanks to him and praise his name." So it is biblical to enter a time of worship with songs of thanks and praise and to celebrate God for who He is and what He has done.

We also see that the psalmists wrote songs of intimacy, expressing their love and adoration to God and marveling at who He is. This is such an important aspect of the journey of worship. God longs for us to pour out our hearts to Him. When you are preparing to lead, pursue God's heart for that service or time of worship, and ask Him to reveal the journey He wants to lead you on. Sometimes I ask and get a sense of where He is leading straightaway, and other times it takes a few days of asking. So be patient, and keep asking.

Tip: If you are preparing to lead worship for a church service or a small group that will involve some kind of teaching, it can be helpful to find out what topic and Bible passage the speaker will be teaching on. You don't always have to choose songs that are consistent with what the speaker is going to teach, but it is helpful to bear it in mind as you prepare. It is also important to find out whether the service you are preparing for will include Communion or anything different from what your church services normally include.

Step 2: Choose your set list

When you have an idea about the journey on which God wants to lead you in that time of worship, the next step is to look at what songs and themes fit. It's important to think about what the songs are saying lyrically and to choose songs of sound biblical doctrine as well as simple songs of intimacy. We need to keep a healthy balance, because the songs we sing often shape our views of God. We also need to consider tempo and how the songs will flow musically and thematically into one another.

Tip: Create a master song list. Something I have found really helpful in this process is having a list of all the songs I know. The song list I created has three columns: one for the title of the song, one for the author, and one for the key. This allows me to see all the song options in front of me.

Here are some things I have learned over the years that are helpful to bear in mind when choosing your set list:

Flow

I have found that putting a couple of songs in the same key after one another can make for a smooth transition. It enables you to go straight from one song to the next, and it avoids having a space of silence between every song in the set. This can help keep people engaged and enable the time of worship to flow well. However, doing too many songs in the same key can become a bit bland—just as doing a set list of five songs in the same tempo could become monotonous—so don't overdo it!

Keeping worship fresh

Are there certain songs that have been used a lot at your church? If so …

- Try giving a song time out. Look at what songs have been used lately. If you find a song has been used a lot in recent weeks, it might be better to let it rest for a week or two. Or, if you think you should keep it in, consider using a new arrangement.

- Introduce some new songs. A new song can transform and breathe life into a time of worship. I have found it really helpful to put a song that the church is familiar with before and after the new one in the set. Those of us who are musical usually find it pretty easy to pick up on new songs, but for most people it takes a few times of hearing it to feel comfortable singing it. As you lead, the congregation has to focus more on learning the words and melody, so I have found that the time of worship flows better if there aren't two unfamiliar songs in a row. Otherwise it can feel like you have lost people, and it takes them awhile to engage again.

Tip: When thinking about using new songs, it's always a good idea to run them by your worship pastor (or pastor, if you are in a small church). Using new songs can bring great freshness to worship, but we need to make sure that they are theologically sound, are congregationally friendly, and will be followed up by the other worship leaders at your church. Unless a song is used consistently for a few weeks, the church will find it hard to learn, and you'll find it difficult to know whether it's really catching on or not. Involving your worship pastor will help guide you in your selection process and make it more likely that other worship leaders are onboard.

- Use different resources. If you tend to use songs written by Hillsong worship leaders, step out and use songs written by Passion worship leaders. If you tend to use songs written by Vineyard worship leaders, try songs written by Soul Survivor worship leaders. These are just suggestions—there are so many great worship songs out there from many other worship leaders and churches, but my point is: Mix it up! This can bring freshness to a time of worship.

- Try fresh band arrangements for familiar songs. A new arrangement can totally change the vibe of a song and bring freshness to a time of worship. So be creative! (We'll look at how to do this at the end of the chapter.)

In all of this, remember there are no rules. You have to go on the journey you feel led to take and choose the songs you feel led to choose.

Women and song choice

I worked for Soul Survivor Ministries for a few years as one of their worship pastors. One of the benefits of this position was that it put me in contact with worship leaders and pastors from lots of different churches. During this time I received an email from a male worship pastor in the US asking me whether I ever led celebration songs, because the female worship leader at his church led only slow and more intimate songs. He wasn't sure whether that was okay for women or whether he should challenge her to learn celebration songs too.

It's true: Over the years I have noticed that women have a tendency to write more intimate songs and use them when they lead. They will often play up-tempo celebration songs more slowly or even avoid them altogether. When I first started leading, I was definitely more drawn to such songs. Other girls have often told me that they don't feel comfortable doing up-tempo songs because they struggle with the rhythm or tempo, especially when trying to play their instrument. If you think of all the songs you know written by women, many of them will be intimate songs of praise. These songs are wonderful and valuable in leading God's people in worship. But when I realized that the songs I knew were quite limited in variety, I made a conscious effort to learn up-tempo praise and celebration songs.

Try some variety in your song choices. As worship leaders it is really important that we pick our set lists from a well-rounded pool of songs. Although we may naturally gravitate toward using one type of song, we should be ready to use a variety when we lead. While it's important to be true to ourselves, we have to be ready to lead people where the Holy Spirit is leading us. A time of celebration won't really happen if we only know songs of lament. Then again—it goes both ways: It will be difficult to lead people into a time of intimacy if we only know songs like "Dancing Generation" by Matt Redman! Remember that as women we bring a different type of sensitivity to worship, so lead out of that place, and choose songs that express this part of who you are. But if you find yourself using only slow, intimate songs, like I did, make sure you learn songs with a variety of themes, tempos, and styles to enable you to take people on the journey of worship that God is leading you on.

Tip: Practice! Whether you play an instrument or not, make sure you are practicing up-tempo songs. Play or sing along to CDs, and if you play an instrument, practice singing and playing them at the same time. If you do not lead on an instrument, get together with a musician from your church regularly to practice. If you are struggling with playing or singing these songs, I promise it will get easier the more you practice!

Step 3: Print out the chord charts/music

When you have figured out your set list, the next step is to print out the chord charts for the songs to provide music for the band. However, for many women it isn't as easy as just printing them out from a worship Web site or photocopying them from a songbook. We have an extra challenge.

Changing the key

One obstacle you are likely to come across when it comes time to organize the chord charts is that a lot of songs are not in a key that suits your vocal range because they are written by men. Let's look at why men's and women's voices are different, so you can explain this to your male pastor or worship pastor.

The different vocal ranges men and women have is one of the more obvious differences you will notice when we lead worship. When the men lead in a key that's comfortable for them, the women often have to sing the melody incredibly low or ear-piercingly high. I have had lots of girls come up to me at events in the past saying that they totally lost their voices from singing along with the guys. And, of course, the same goes when women lead: The men complain about having to sing really low or really high.

The changes in a girl's voice when she is growing up are barely noticeable—they go down one or two tones. However, as a guy grows up, his vocal chords get thicker, they grow 60 percent longer, and this makes his vocal chords vibrate at a lower frequency than before. While this change takes place, his voice box tilts to a different angle, which is why the Adam's apple appears. Meanwhile, his face changes a lot during this time—the bones grow bigger, and as the facial structure changes, it makes more room for the sound to resonate, which makes the voice sound lower.[1]

How our different vocal ranges affect worship

When men lead worship, they lead in a key that is comfortable for them, and that is totally right! Women may struggle to sing the melody at times, but it would be ridiculous to expect a male worship leader to sing in a key that is uncomfortable for him. Some women have worked out how to harmonize so they can sing the songs comfortably. But those who can't harmonize may struggle to sing along, which can make engaging with God through sung worship difficult at times.

Although our differences may make singing together a challenge, they really are a wonderful thing. They drive us to harmonize and create beautiful sounds using our different tones and vocal ranges. When we sing together, the male and female voices complement one another beautifully.

Change the key!

So the obvious thing to say is—feel free to change the key! You may think it goes without saying, but many girls don't actually know they can do this and just struggle on. Also, from what girls have told me, many male worship pastors expect them to sing in the same key as the men. I have led seminars where, even after I've explained why girls' and guys' voices are different, guys have come up to me still not getting it. One man said that when the women in his worship team say they can't physically sing what he is expecting them to, he tells them to just step back from the mic and really belt it out. That is a one-way road to discouraged female worship leaders with damaged vocal chords! Definitely not a good idea.

Find the right key for your vocal range

Let's look at this practically. When you want to learn a new song, get your instrument, or find someone who plays an instrument, and work out what key best suits your voice for that song. For me, this has been trial and error, and you may have to try a couple of different keys before you find the right one for you. Remember that your vocal health is the first priority, because if you damage your voice by pushing it too much, you won't be able to lead at all. Bear in mind, though, that it's different for each individual vocalist. There are many women who have greater vocal ranges than mine. I am never going to hit the notes that Mariah Carey reaches! She has a gift—and had intense vocal training as a child. So don't listen to other women and kill yourself trying to lead a song in the same key. Find a key that is comfortable for you.

Tip: Warm up and stand up. When you are in the process of working out what key suits your vocal range, make sure you have warmed up your voice and you aren't sitting down on your couch! I used to try to work out the keys for songs sitting down and without warming up, and would then go to band practice and discover that I could bump the songs up a key or two. We sing very differently on the couch at home than when we're standing in front of a microphone.

Get some training

It is so important to know your voice. If you find that your vocal range is quite limited, which is definitely where I started, it's important to get singing lessons to help stretch your vocal range. Practice and practice, and then practice some more. The more you sing, the more comfortable you'll become with your voice and how to use and control it. You are also likely to find that the more you lead, the more your vocal range will naturally stretch. This has been the case with me. There are many songs I used to sing in lower keys that I have bumped up, and there are a few songs that I have taken down a key. I was always straining to sing them, so I made that change. Again, it was trial and error for a while, but now the process is a lot easier because I know my own voice better.

Serve the men in your church as best as you can

In all this, try to be mindful of the men in your church, and do your best to choose as high a key as you can in order to make it comfortable for them. Our aim is to balance what works for both sexes. In reality, women will find it easier to sing with women, and men will find it easier to sing with men, but we need to make worship as accessible as we can for both men and women when we lead.

Songs you may struggle to sing

Because girls' and guys' vocal ranges are different, I can't sing certain songs, or at least sections of songs, written by guys. For example, Tim Hughes' song "Everything" has an octave jump, and Matt Redman's song "Nothing but the Blood" jumps from a low verse to a high chorus. If I were to try to lead these songs, I would have to either sing the verses so low that you could barely hear me or leave out the jumps, which then would take away a lot of the songs' energy. Personally, I have tended to just leave those songs to the men or use songs like "Everything" in ministry time where it's probably more appropriate to keep it chilled and not do the octave jump.

Some women can sing these songs because they can naturally sing higher than me and sound great, but I have totally struggled with them over the years. So just be aware that you may come across this when you are learning new songs. But please don't lose hope. When I started leading worship, I couldn't sing some songs that I now really enjoy singing. Sometimes reaching the notes can be a bit of a push, but remember your range will improve the more you lead. It can be frustrating at times, because there are some really fantastic songs that you may struggle to lead because of your range, but it's just part of being different!

Tip: Ask others to sing with you. One female worship leader told me that she often asks a backing vocalist to sing the melody with her if she is struggling to hit a note herself. This is a great idea if you want to use a song without leaving sections out. She said that having someone else sing with her gives her more confidence to sing out and gives more support to the melody if she does struggle to hit some notes. It may work best to get a *male* backing vocalist to sing with you, because if you're struggling to hit a note, it's likely that other females will too. A male backing vocalist's vocal tone and range will likely complement your female vocal tone and range and will give you great support when singing the melody.

Key change and backing vocals

Changing the key to a song will affect the backing vocals. For example, a man might have two female singers, both singing different harmonies when they lead. But when I lead the same song, because I have taken the key down, one of the harmonies becomes too low. So often I just have one female backing vocalist, or a guy and a girl—which also works really well. Some female singers have a range and tone that sound great when they sing above the melody I am singing—but they need to sing that harmony sensitively, because it will be quite high.

Don't get stressed if you don't fully understand how key change can affect backing vocals. There are many great resources out there that can help you cover the technical aspects of harmonies, but it's just something to be aware of when changing the key.

Resources

When I first started leading worship, I wondered why there wasn't a songbook with chord charts that suited women's voices—I thought it would make things so much easier. But as I mentioned before, many women have different ranges and lead songs in different keys, so it would be difficult to have one songbook that suits *all* women.

As someone who has limited knowledge of music theory, I often use a program that any church can subscribe to on the Christian Copyright Licensing International Web site (CCLI.com) called SongSelect. SongSelect allows you to search for a song, choose the key, and print out the resulting chord chart. It's a great resource. However, one of the downsides of SongSelect is that you can't download the charts—you can only print them out. So in order to have the songs permanently on my computer, I created Microsoft Word documents for many of the chord charts in the keys I sing them in. It has meant that I have access to them on my laptop wherever I go—which is especially helpful if you don't have Internet access.

Always remember that, for the duplication and distribution of chord charts for your church worship team to be legal, you need to make sure you have permission from the publisher of each song. If your church has a Church Copyright License, then you are free to create Word documents, duplicate, and distribute any songs covered by it.[2] If a song is not covered by it, you will need to contact the song's publisher directly to request permission.

The Kingsway Web site (www.kingsway.co.uk) also has a great resource that allows you to purchase the chord chart you want, change the key to suit your vocal range, and download that song to your computer, which is very helpful and saves you the time it takes to create Word documents.

All of these tools are there to make things easier, but it is a good idea to learn some music theory so that you understand how to transpose music. Below is a chart I have used that has taught me what chords are in each key and has really helped me to transpose songs:

Key	1	2	3	4	5	6	7
C	C	Dm	Em	F	G	Am	Bdim
D	D	Em	F#m	G	A	Bm	C#dim
Eb	Eb	Fm	Gm	Ab	Bb	Cm	Ddim
E	E	F#m	G#m	A	B	C#m	D#dim
F	F	Gm	Am	Bb	C	Dm	Edim
G	G	Am	Bm	C	D	Em	F#dim
Ab	Ab	Bbm	Cm	Db	Eb	Fm	Gdim
A	A	Bm	C#m	D	E	F#m	G#dim
Bb	Bb	Cm	Dm	Eb	F	Gm	Adim
B	B	C#m	D#m	E	F#	G#m	A#dim

Not every key is represented in this chart. I have simplified it and included most of the keys that you will find worship songs

written in. (Don't worry too much about the 7 chord in each
key—diminished chords are rarely used in contemporary worship
music.)

At first glance this may just look like a lot of chord names.
However, it really is quite a simple chart that makes transposing keys
easy. As you can see in the chart, every chord is represented by a
number, so all the chords in the column titled "1" are the 1 chords
in their respective key and so on. If the song you want to transpose is
in the key of C, the 1 chord is a C. The rows represent all the chords
in that key. So in the key of C, for example, the chords in that key
are C, Dm, Em, F, G, Am, and Bdim. Now that we know the layout
of the chart, let's transpose a song. As an example, we will use the
first few lines of the song "Happy Day"[3] by Tim Hughes and Ben
Cantelon and transpose it from the key of C to the key of G so that
we can sing it lower. Here are the first few lines in the key of C (the
men's key):

C

The greatest day in history—

F   Am

Death is beaten, you have rescued me;

                                                  F

Sing it out: Jesus is alive!

We can go to the chart and see that in the key of C, the C is
the 1 chord. To transpose it to G, we need to go to the line where
G is the 1 chord. So in the song, replace the C with the G. The next
chord is an F, and we can see that in the key of C, the F chord is
the 4 chord. In the key of G, we can see from the chart that the 4
chord is a C, so we then substitute the F for a C. Am (the *m* stands

for minor) in the key of C is the 6 chord, and in the key of G, the 6 chord is an Em, so we then replace the Am with an Em. We've already established that the F is changed to a C, and we can see that to play the first few lines of "Happy Day" in the key of G (the key I lead it in), the chord chart would look like this:

G

The greatest day in history—

C   Em

Death is beaten, you have rescued me;

C

Sing it out: Jesus is alive!

Don't worry if you're finding the chart hard to fully understand at first. If you can, just meet up with a friend who knows music theory so they can go through it with you and explain it further. Once you get it, you'll find it really easy to transpose the song you want to use into a key that suits your vocal range.

Step 4: Band arrangements

Once you've printed out all the chord charts for the songs in your set list, the next step is to look at the arrangements for the songs. Band arrangements not only create dynamics for the songs, but they also avoid relying on each musician to interpret the song and guess where you are going. Without band arrangements things could get pretty messy. I am not suggesting that the main goal is to make the music perfect. Of course the goal is worshipping God. But God has given us these musical gifts, and it's right that we practice and do our best to prepare practically. Music communicates so much, and we have this amazing opportunity to use music to help lead people in worship.

What are band dynamics?

If you listen to a live recording of a song, you will be able to hear certain instruments and voices more prominently at times and less at others. The use of volume changes and instrumentation in band arrangements creates dynamics, as though layers are being added and taken away. It's important to use band arrangements for each song, because they give the music texture and movement and enable you to reflect the lyrics and style. To help explain band dynamics better, let's look at an example of an arrangement of "Blessed Be Your Name"[4] by Matt and Beth Redman.

Intro: The song starts with the drummer clicking in and every instrument playing the chorus chords. The electric guitarist drives the intro. This creates energy and reflects the song's theme of praise.

Verse 1: The electric guitar drops out, and the drummer continues to play along with the bass guitarist. The keys player plays pads, and the acoustic guitarist strums out chords. The electric guitarist drops out of the verse so that you have somewhere to go when you want the song to sound bigger, for example, in the chorus.

Pre-chorus: The drummer, bass guitarist, keys player, and acoustic guitarist continue to play, and the electric guitarist now comes in with a simple part while the backing vocals begin to sing. This starts building the song and leads nicely into the chorus.

Chorus: Much like the intro, everyone is playing with great energy, plus the backing vocals are singing with the worship leader. When everyone is in, it emphasizes this section of the song.

Verse 2: (Same as verse 1)

Chorus: (Same as the previous chorus)

Bridge: The band pulls back and minimizes what they are playing, and the drummer begins to build. Gradually the instruments and voices build with the drummer, and by the end of the bridge everyone is playing and singing. This creates tension and will lead strongly into a high-energy chorus.

Chorus: Everyone is playing with great energy, the backing vocals are singing, and the song ends strongly.

The arrangements you choose will totally depend on what type of song it is and what you want to communicate with that song. "Blessed Be Your Name" is a song of praise that speaks of trusting God and worshipping Him through all seasons of life, so the arrangement for this song reflects praise. But when leading an intimate song of love for Jesus, you'd take a different approach: You probably wouldn't start with the drummer clicking into a high-energy chorus, for one thing! In that case, you may start the song more gently in order to reflect the intimacy of the lyrics. Definitely pay attention to the lyrics of the song, and keep them in mind when choosing an arrangement.

Use band arrangements that reflect the musicianship of the band

There are so many creative ways to arrange a song, but obviously these need to be within your band's own musical limits. Choose arrangements that suit your band and play to your strengths. If you have a really strong electric guitarist, use that strength. If your keys player is not that strong, don't start every song with the keys or give the player too many specific parts. Think about who is in the band, and play to their strengths. If you have a bunch of newer musicians, keep it simple. If you have more experienced musicians, you can try more complicated arrangements.

Listening to CDs of worship songs can really help give you ideas for band arrangements. However, many of the people who play on these CDs are very experienced musicians, and sometimes these arrangements can be too difficult for the musicians in most churches. So if you feel your band might not be able to pull it off, simplify it.

Here are a few things that may help you when choosing band arrangements:

- The opening of the first song is important. Consult the service leader to avoid a situation where he or she opens with a psalm of lament and the band comes crashing in with a song like "Happy Day." It's always helpful to communicate with the service leader so everyone can be on the same page.

- It can be really helpful to go over the intros to the songs at the end of band practice. This helps avoid train-wrecking the beginning of songs, and it gives the musicians confidence, because generally once the song has started, people remember the rest.

- Think how you are going to link songs musically. If you keep finishing a song softly but then come crashing into the next song, the time of worship will probably be up and down and maybe even give people a bit of a fright! If the previous song ended gently, try starting the next song by yourself on guitar or keys (depending on what you play), or if you don't lead on an instrument, ask another band member to start the song for you. The keys player playing pads is also a great way to have smooth transitions while keeping momentum. It also enables the guitarists to change capo if necessary without awkward silences. Of course silence can be part of a time of worship, but pads can help when you are not intending silence.

• Don't be afraid to keep a song totally "down" the whole time. Not every song has to build to a crescendo. Building can create great dynamics and can emphasize a section of a song, but if you do that in every song, it may begin to lose its impact and become exhausting to the worshippers.

• If you feel the Holy Spirit leading you in a different direction from the one you practiced with the band (e.g., you feel you need to take things down when you had originally planned to start with the drummer clicking in with the whole band), make sure you communicate this clearly to the rest of the band. Communicate to the drummer not to click in and that you are going to start the song yourself. Use your signals to be clear in where you are going (see chapter 4). As frustrating as changing it up may be for some musicians, it's more important that we follow where the Holy Spirit is leading than sticking to what we practiced. We just need to be clear and lead strongly in these times.

Step 5: Leading band practice

When you arrive at church for band practice, give the set list and the chord charts to the band before you begin to practice the songs (obviously the set list and chord charts are subject to change if you feel something is not working during band practice). I usually start with a familiar song because it's just a good way to ease the band in. Using a familiar song means that they can play through it confidently, which makes it easier for the sound guy to adjust the levels and for the electric guitarist to play around with their pedals to get the sound they want to achieve.

I usually give a brief explanation of what I would like each song arrangement to be and then practice that song a couple of times, and so on for each song. I make sure I am communicating with the musicians, encouraging them if I love what they are playing, but also being honest if I am not sure it works or if I would prefer them to play something else. Don't be afraid to be honest—just make sure you communicate with kindness and encourage them. It makes all the difference.

Making choices

When leading band practice, you are going to have to make choices. You may be playing with musicians who are more advanced than you, and it can be quite challenging at times to know when to stick with the musical ideas you have chosen and when to take their advice if they have a different suggestion. My husband, Paul, is usually in the band when I am leading, and he also leads worship and plays every instrument that you would find in a worship band. However, despite how talented he is, because we are two different people, we don't always agree. He might disagree with my choice of song, or I may not like an arrangement he suggests. Sometimes I trust his judgment and go with his advice, but other times I choose to go with my idea. However, there have been times when it's been difficult to be confident in what I want to do because he is more musically advanced than I am. I have found it hard to know whether his advice or opinion is based on his preference because of his personal taste or because my idea actually doesn't work as well. In these situations I just weigh it up. We usually practice the song both ways, and then I decide what I feel works better. Making this kind of decision is all part of leading!

Endnotes

1. "Puberty," Science & Nature: Human Body & Mind, BBC.com, www.bbc.co.uk/science/humanbody/body/articles/lifecycle/teenagers/voice.shtml (accessed November 16, 2009).

2. To find out whether a song is covered by CCLI, go to www.ccli.com and enter the appropriate song information in the "Song Search" section. If the song you have searched for is covered by them, you will need to include all copyright information and your CCLI license number on each chord chart. For more information, read CCLI's "License Manual" on their Web site.

3. Tim Hughes and Ben Cantelon, "Happy Day," *Holding Nothing Back* © 2006 Thankyou Music.

4. Matt and Beth Redman, "Blessed Be Your Name," *Where Angels Fear to Tread* © 2002 Thankyou Music.

6

Leading a band

Working as a team can be tough. Just because we are Christians and part of a team that's formed to lead people in worshipping a holy God doesn't mean we lose our humanity. We come to that team with our insecurities, our brokenness, and our weaknesses. With that in mind, let's look at the characteristics that will make us good bandleaders.

Communication

To lead people confidently, communication is key. It is hugely important in creating an atmosphere where the band members feel safe and valued and can follow the worship leader easily. The team needs to feel that they can ask questions, and the worship leader needs to be clear in communicating his or her vision for the worship time, the songs he or she wants to use, the keys the songs are in, and all the other little details. This will enable people to jump onboard with the vision and bring their creativity to that band practice.

Communicate creative ideas and arrangements

I cannot tell you the amount of times I have tried to suggest a certain drumbeat to the drummer, or a style to another musician, and they really had no idea what I was talking about. There have been some funny moments, but it's also been frustrating for me and for them at times because I just haven't had the language to communicate clearly with them in musical terms. If you feel like you need help with this, get together with stronger musicians and ask them questions so that you understand more and better communicate with the band members.

There is a lot of room to involve the musicians in creative decisions as well, so ask the band if they have any ideas. Everyone can bring something different, and his or her creative ideas can bring such freshness to the worship time. It's up to you whether you take their suggestions further or not, but it's great for them to have that outlet, and it can really benefit the time of worship.

Communicate practically

We need to communicate clearly with the band during band practice and also during the time of worship. Musicians long for a worship leader who is easy to follow, so you need to have some signals that communicate clearly what you want the band to do. In chapter 4, Kathryn, Christy, and I shared some of the signals we use, and you may find they work for you, too. However, you can use whatever signals you are comfortable with—it doesn't matter what they are as long as they are consistent and visible to the whole band.

Communicate pastorally

The worship leader also needs to communicate with the band pastorally—this can mean no more than asking how their week was or how they feel about their musical setup or monitor mix. And don't forget the backing vocalists. I have sung backing vocals when the worship leader talked often with the musicians but neglected to communicate with the backing vocalists—it was as though we weren't really part of the band. We had no direction and weren't sure when to come in and when not to sing. It wasn't intentional, but the leader was just a lot more focused on what the drummer was doing, for example, and was unaware of how it made us feel. (When we told the leader, we were immediately treated like any other band member.)

Confidence

Every worship leader has a different personality. Some may be young, some older. But one characteristic a band wants in every worship leader is confidence. Someone who is humble, seeks God, and has a sense of how to lead people to the place God wants them to go.

I am young, I am a woman, and I am often surrounded by older, more talented male musicians. But God has really challenged me not to be intimidated by this fact. I've got to trust that He has put me in this position and that I can be confident in my ability to hear Him and sense where He wants to take His people.

When I was leading worship at an event a few years ago, I came to band practice knowing that in about an hour and a half, twelve thousand people would come flooding through the doors. All I could think was, *Oh my goodness, what were they thinking when they decided to put me up here?* On top of all the thoughts going through my mind, I had to lead a band practice full of very skilled musicians who were all men. It was terrifying in many ways.

After we had started to practice one of the songs, I soon realized that I didn't really like the sound the keyboardist was playing. He was playing quite an electronic sound, but the song was quite intimate, and I wanted a piano sound. So I kindly asked him if he could make the change. But one of the other band members overheard my request and said he thought the original sound was fine. At that point it would have been easy for me to lose confidence in my opinion and just leave it and have him play the original sound. But I decided to say that it would be great if he could try a piano sound … please.

Inevitably, whether the musicians in the band were more musical than I was or not, or whether they agreed with my decision or not, as the worship leader I had the authority to go with what I felt worked best. And no one thought anything more about it. If the worship leader lacks confidence, the band won't feel confident in following him or her. It's important to go with what you feel is best and be confident in your decisions. Just remember to step out in confidence with humility and kindness.

Encouragement

We all need encouragement, and members of the band are no different. If we point out only the things we don't like about what they play or sing, they will feel insecure.

Encourage them when they have done well, and when you're not doing that, remember to thank them for the time they give. Make a special effort with new band members, but bear in mind that even those who have been on the team for a long time still need encouragement. When people are encouraged, they thrive.

Developing your skill

We will also lead the band better the more musical we are. It's important that as worship leaders we pursue growing in our skills. Our musicianship must not get in the way of our leading worship, but rather facilitate it and give us a firm foundation from which to lead. As we grow in our skills, we will be able to communicate more clearly to the band, understand the other musicians better, and lead more confidently.

Spirit-led worship

In these last two chapters, we have looked at many of the practical aspects of preparing to lead worship, but there is of course a spiritual aspect, too. It says in John 4:24 that "God is spirit, and his worshipers must worship in spirit and in truth," so we must seek to be led by His Holy Spirit—both when we worship Him and when we are preparing to lead worship. What does this mean?

Although we plan and prepare our set list and songs, we are to be open and ready to move in whatever direction we sense the Holy Spirit leading. Our God speaks today, He moves today, and we must be open to His Spirit leading us as we seek to lead the congregation. Worship is so much more exciting when we allow God to have His way!

Now I realize that, depending on what your experience is and what church you go to, this can be easier said than done. The church my husband and I work for in Florida is filled with people from different church backgrounds. Some have come from very conservative churches, where worship has been led by one musician playing the organ, so just the fact that we lead on guitar and have a full band is totally new for them. Simply coming to our church causes them to step out of their comfort zone. Others have come from charismatic backgrounds and are used to extended times of worship and the gifts of the Spirit. Meanwhile, others have come from churches where, although worship is led with a full band playing contemporary worship songs, they are not comfortable with there being any spontaneity during the service.

Diversity is one of our strengths as a church, but it makes leading worship tricky sometimes. We want to make people feel safe when they have stepped out. We want the whole church to join as one as we worship God. This means finding a balance between stepping out and following where we sense that the Holy Spirit is leading, while creating a safe environment for those who are new to the church. We don't want to "go for it" if that means leaving people behind; yet, we also don't want to hold back from following where the Holy Spirit is leading just because we are trying to make sure everyone feels comfortable. This is the balancing act we must perform in our journey together as we lead worship.

A few years ago I went to Disney's California Adventure theme park with a couple of friends. I was really excited about going on the rides, so when my friends suggested the roller coaster, I was totally up for it! Little did I know that things had changed since the last time I had been on one. Instead of a gentle ride on wooden tracks, I sat in a high-tech roller coaster that shot out like a rocket with terrifying twists, turns, and tunnels. To make things worse, my two friends were sitting together behind me, and I was on my own. I was in total shock the whole ride. I was so terrified that I was holding on for dear life and couldn't even scream. At one point I looked back at my friends, and they were roaring with laughter, throwing their arms up in the air and having the time of their lives. My experience was totally different. It took me about half an hour to recover after I got off and consoled myself with the thought that I was never going on a roller coaster again!

For some, the experience of church can feel like my wild ride on that roller coaster. Recently when I was leading worship, I left some space in a song where the band kept playing and I just sang out the name of Jesus. It wasn't on the lyrics screen because it was a spontaneous moment. To me it was totally normal. It was just a simple melody, and I was singing out the name of our Savior, encouraging others to sing out what was on their hearts as they felt led. I believed that it had been a really lovely moment, but after church I was told that someone had brought a friend who was totally freaked out by it. I was gutted. I had tried to be obedient, and I didn't really understand why it was so scary for this person. I mean, if they were at a sporting event and people began shouting, singing out, or cheering spontaneously, they probably wouldn't have thought anything of it. But then God reminded me of being on that roller coaster. I realized that some people come expecting it to be church the way they are used to. So when something different happens, they react and may even be terrified, just like I was on that roller coaster: They look at others in the church really enjoying it and think they are totally crazy! They leave the service thinking, *Never again!* The worst-case scenario is that they can totally shut down to the Holy Spirit, choosing to stay within their comfort zone.

Finding the balance can be really hard because it's like walking a tightrope. After I received the feedback about that person (which was not the first time), I felt discouraged. Leading worship makes you so vulnerable, especially when you step out and take a risk like that. It was a little while after that experience that I realized I had shut down and was leading on autopilot. Part of me felt so discouraged that somewhere along the line I just started going from A to B, giving the congregation what I thought they wanted to avoid being criticized.

Thankfully my husband sat me down one day and told me to "get over myself" (cheeky, I know!) and to stop holding back. He challenged me to keep going for it, being obedient to what I felt God was saying. That may sound a bit harsh, but he was totally right. Something shifted in that moment, and I was reminded that worship becomes dry when we shut ourselves down to the Holy Spirit. The thing I loved had become something I dreaded, because I was functioning out of a fear of what people were thinking.

I needed to do my best to pastor those in the congregation, and I also needed to be obedient to God. Successfully leading in this way all comes down to communication. Now I always explain what is going on in order to help people feel safe when they are out of their comfort zone. My hope is that, over time, those in the congregation will begin to trust me and will become more open to responding to God as His Spirit leads us.

So if, like me, you are in an environment where doing anything spontaneous or off script might be new to people, it is a great idea for either you or the service leader to explain what is going on. For example, I might say that there is a song on my heart and I feel I should sing it out, and I encourage the congregation to just receive. Or I encourage them to sing their own songs to God and for us to join together in singing whatever is on our hearts.

I know that in some situations it can be distracting if the worship leader speaks a lot during a time of worship, but I have realized that there are times when I will lead people better if I say something, whether it's using Scripture or just explaining where I sense God leading. It can also be helpful if the service leader explains things at the end of a time of worship. It just means that if someone is at your church for the first time, he or she will know what's going on, and that in itself creates a sense of safety.

If you are from a church where the congregation is used to spontaneous worship and changing things up in response to where you feel the Holy Spirit is leading, I want to challenge you to equip yourself to lead in different environments. You never know where God might open a door for you, so it's really important to be able to lead strongly in different contexts. We all need to be sensitive to the environments we are in, aiming to take as many people as possible with us on the journey of worship.

Don't be discouraged if you are in an environment where the spontaneous is not an option. You can still grow and learn to follow where the Holy Spirit is leading in your personal times of worship, remembering that the Holy Spirit is the one leading us as we prepare our worship sets too.

Lastly, I want to encourage you not to be afraid to get it wrong. The only way to learn to hear God's voice and follow His Spirit is to give it a go. We aren't always going to get it right. That's okay. It's better to take the risk than to play it safe all the time and miss out on the things that God may want to do during a time of worship.

Having said that, however, please don't feel a pressure to make things happen. Many of us fall into this because it's easy to feel that worship is more special if something spontaneous happens. But that's not the case at all. We know that the Holy Spirit leads us as we prepare as well as in the service itself, which means that it's perfectly okay if nothing unplanned happens. I usually stick to what I've planned unless I get a really strong sense that I should do something different, which may or may not happen.

Go with wherever you feel God leading, including when you prepare your set, and be encouraged knowing that no matter what happens, He loves you and is for you. He is cheering you on in your journey of learning to follow His Spirit.

7

Working with your pastor

One of the main people you are likely to work with when leading worship is your pastor. Often your pastor will be leading or overseeing the church services, and it's important that you work well together. Let's look at how we can best serve them and work together.

Work together

Pastors long for worship leaders who have a heart for God, the church, and working together—all before "their own ministry." I have come across worship leaders who feel frustrated when their pastors make comments or suggestions about the worship. They feel as though worship is "their time," and they don't want the pastors to "cut in." However, it's not our time, it's God's time, and those in leadership over us have the authority during services. Although as worship leaders we lead most of the musical side of things, it is important for us to trust our pastor's judgment. It can be hard at times to tell what's going on in the congregation when you're onstage, so our pastor's input from worshipping as part of the congregation gives us a different perspective that will help us lead the congregation better.

Basically, this is how it works for me: When I am leading, my pastor and I often talk before the service to discuss anything we feel God has been speaking to us about for that service or any direction we feel He is moving in. We keep open lines of communication during the service too. There have been times when we have come to the end of our planned set and I sense that God is doing something, and I will signal to my pastor to come over so I can quietly communicate this to him. He then weighs it up and communicates to the congregation if need be.

At other times I may come to the end of a planned set, and he might signal to keep going, and then the band keeps playing until he signals to stop or closes that time of worship with a prayer.

There have also been times when he has suggested a song he feels we should sing. You may think it strange for a pastor to suggest a song, but we need to remember that most church leaders are passionate worshippers whether they themselves are musicians or not. They have lots of experience of listening to the Holy Spirit and often have great suggestions.

We need to humble ourselves and recognize that we don't know everything about leading worship. We weren't created to work alone. We are called to work together and will lead with greater strength when we work *with* our pastors. We need to submit to them "out of reverence for Christ" (Ephesians 5:21). Submitting to them means honoring them no matter what and deferring to their leadership.

Honoring those in authority over us is not always easy. The reality is that there will be times when we don't see eye to eye. However, we need to remember that we are looking at the church service with our focus on the time of worship, but our pastor or service leader is looking at the big picture of the whole service and vision for the church. So it's crucial that we trust their judgment and defer to their leadership. It's not that we can't ask questions, make suggestions, or disagree, but it's important that we choose to be obedient to them and privately and publicly support them and their decisions, because this pleases the Lord.

In my experience the best pastors lead strongly yet are also incredibly releasing, allowing their worship leaders to step out and take risks. I am very fortunate that the pastors I have worked with have given me freedom to go for it and have told me that it's okay to make mistakes. Environments like this allow us to grow, because we learn to lead so much better without fear of failure or the pressure to get it right every time. Deferring to your pastor's leadership is both important and biblical, and as they release us and we submit to them, we are serving "one another in love" (Galatians 5:13).

This next section, "Working with your male pastor," is for both you and your male pastor to read.

Working with your male pastor

Ladies, I am sure that many of you have at times felt as though you are on the sidelines, while the male worship leaders are getting all the investment from your male pastor. And, pastors, I know that many of you want to get alongside female worship leaders but just don't know how. Many pastors have never had to work with women in this way before, so you aren't totally sure how to relate to them. We are very different from men, and I can imagine that this seems daunting for you at times. But it's good to look at the relationship between a female worship leader and her male pastor, so we can learn how to understand each other better and work well together.

First, I want to address the male pastor and look at some of the fears and challenges you may face when it comes to investing in female worship leaders. I want to help you find healthy ways to encourage, equip, and empower the women at your church who are called to lead worship.

Emotions

One of the main concerns male pastors have voiced when I have spoken with them about training up female worship leaders is that they are worried that we are going to respond emotionally if they challenge us. It is true—women tend to be more emotional than men. There have been a couple of times in the past when I've been challenged and have cried, and I am sure I am not the only woman who has responded like this. For many women, it's similar to laughing when someone tells a joke—we cry sometimes when we find something difficult or upsetting. So please don't be afraid of tears.

I am in no way saying that it's okay if one of your female worship leaders cries hysterically every time you challenge her or give her constructive feedback, though. If anyone responds like that consistently, it would seem that there is something deeper that needs to be dealt with, and I would definitely encourage that woman to meet with someone who could help her work through whatever it is that's causing her dramatic response. But tears are just something you may come across when working with women, and they are okay!

One thing you need to know is that you are not responsible for dealing with the emotional side of things. Your job is to invest in the female worship leaders at your church and train them as best as you can, which will include constructive criticism at times, and it's their responsibility to process this with one of their female friends or their spouse.

Tip: One thing to remember is that it's all about delivery. Women are usually more sensitive than men, so just remember to be kind and encouraging when you give constructive feedback. It will make all the difference!

Healthy boundaries

I have learned through conversations with male pastors that many of them feel really uncomfortable encouraging women. You will want to guard yourself from any issues that may arise from relating with the opposite sex, and you may fear that we may take your encouragement the wrong way. I totally understand why you feel like this. We all know there are leaders who have found themselves in tricky situations with the opposite sex, so it is fantastic that you want to be on your guard. But your desire to do the right thing does not make it okay to invest only in men and leave the women to fend for themselves. There are ways to appropriately get alongside and invest in the women who God is raising up!

Here are some helpful suggestions:

- Meet at your church with other staff members around, with the door open, or in a room with a glass window.

- Meet in a public setting, such as a coffee shop, and if it would make you feel more comfortable, bring another staff member with you.

- Encourage the women in a band setting. Before or after band practice is a great time to chat to them in an environment you will both be comfortable in.

- Meet with and encourage all your worship leaders in a group setting.

You have to find a way to deal with this issue; you can't avoid encouraging or raising up female worship leaders because it's initially a bit awkward or because it takes more effort. If there is no one to encourage or train them, they are not going to feel supported or believed in, and this will leave them lacking confidence when they lead. In today's world where predominantly men are leading worship, it's crucial that you actively pursue encouraging the women.

You're not alone

Through all of this, know that you are not alone in the challenge of training up the opposite sex. The same thing applies when women in leadership roles are responsible for training and investing in male worship leaders. Imagine if I never sought to train male worship leaders and only sought out female worship leaders, so that our church had only women leading worship. How wrong would that be? The church would miss out on the wonderful things that men bring as they lead worship. The ideal is obviously that churches have both men and women leading worship. I am very excited about seeing women raised up to lead worship, but I am also excited to see men leading too. All of us should be excited to have both men and women leading at our churches and to see God use our differences to lead people into His presence.

And consider this: If you train and invest in female worship leaders now, you won't have to be as involved in training other females in the future. You will have given your current leaders the tools to be able to train the newer female worship leaders themselves. So in the long run it's actually liberating for both you and the women.

Be intentional

Because you are a man, it's likely that you will naturally spot leadership potential in other men, but you may have to be more intentional in seeking out female worship leaders. Ask God if there are any women on your worship team or in your church who He is calling to lead worship, and if He speaks to you, be active in getting them involved when you feel the time is right.

Tip: When seeking to spot in women gifts and anointing for leading worship, it can be really helpful to involve other female leaders and mature believers you know and trust. Ask them whether they have seen potential in anyone, or if you have someone in mind, ask her opinion. Her input will be valuable.

Free them to be themselves

It is also important that you free the female worship leaders you are training to be themselves. Be excited to see them step out and bring something different from the men. Free them to change the key to songs in order to enable them to sing them comfortably. It may not be the most comfortable key for you to sing in, but it's unrealistic to expect someone who has been created differently to have the same vocal range as you.

It can be done well

Lastly, with all of the challenges that arise from working with the opposite sex, I want you to know that there is a lot of hope. It's not always a struggle, and it can be done well. My current pastor, Antley, is amazing. I have always felt just as valuable as the men, as he has encouraged me and released me to be myself. We don't hang out one-on-one, but he still supports me, and I know I can always go and chat with him about any concerns I have if I need to. You have the unique opportunity to be used by God to empower women in all that God has called them to, so go for it! The challenges you face are completely worth it.

I now want to address the female worship leaders and look at some of the things that will enable you to work well with your male pastor.

Facing the facts

One of the realities of being a female worship leader in today's world is that your pastor and worship pastor are more than likely going to be men than women. You are going to have to face the fact that their relationship with you is going to look different from their relationships with the male worship leaders at your church. This can be hard because you almost certainly won't get the same amount of input as them.

In the past I have found this a bit tough. All of us find it scary to step out, and we often feel vulnerable when we lead worship or write new songs. For me it has often felt like a lonely journey. The result is that I have often struggled to feel confident in what I bring to the table as a worship leader. But at the end of the day I have to choose to listen to God's voice of encouragement to me and to remember the things I feel He has created and called me to do. What really motivates me is knowing that, although my journey as a female worship leader has been a lonely one, the more I invest in other female worship leaders and make myself available to them, the more it gives them what I didn't have. As I invest in others, they will in turn invest in those women around them, and that to me is exciting! All of us can be part of this.

The way our male pastor invests in us will look different from how they invest in the men, but that shouldn't make us feel any less valued. Although we are right to expect our male leaders to support us as we grow and step out in our gifts, we need to pursue finding our confidence and affirmation in God alone. And when fear and insecurity rise, we need to hold on to the truth and remember the words in Zephaniah 3:17: "The LORD your God is with you, he is mighty to save. He will take great delight in you, he will quiet you with his love, he will rejoice over you with singing."

As women, our challenge is to find our identity and security in God alone. We don't have to push our way out there to try to prove to the men that we can do it. The Lord will make a way and open the doors. We just have to take the role of a servant—serving both men and women—as we seek to lead people into His presence. God is calling us to be teachable and to step out and be ourselves, because He can use us much more powerfully that way.

8

Songwriting

Earlier I shared how God delights in what we bring to Him in worship—how we bring joy to Him in a way unique to each one of us. This truth has transformed not only the way I worship but also the way I approach songwriting.

It can be so easy to make a subtle yet significant shift here—to somehow switch our focus from writing songs of love, adoration, and praise to Jesus ... to writing songs that others are going to love, adore, and praise.

Of course it's right to want to write songs that others will sing, but as worshippers this cannot be our chief goal. So before we look at the practical side of songwriting, I want to share a couple of fundamentals I have found helpful to bear in mind when getting down to writing songs.

For Him

First, we need to remember that the songs are for Him. It is an amazing thought that all over the world, in different nations, languages, and styles, worshippers are writing songs of worship to God. There must be so many amazing songs out there that none of us will ever hear, but the Lord hears them all. There must also be songs that we have heard and didn't think much of but God absolutely loves. These songs receive no praise on earth, but they bless His heart because He sees the heart of the writer.

This is a wonderful reminder that the value or worth of our songs does not come from what others think—it comes from God, who sees our hearts. It's important to keep our focus on Him and to keep writing out of the overflow of our love for Him. I want to write songs that *He* loves. The opinions of people will always vary depending on personality and taste. There will always be those who like what you write and those who don't, so don't let your goal be to please others. Your heart's desire must be to please God.

Take the pressure off

We also need to take the pressure off ourselves. When we read the Psalms, we see that David wrote songs to God as a response to who He is and what He has done; and he also wrote about what was going on in his life. This blend of personal revelation of God with life experience reads at times almost like a journal.

We see David's heart expressed to God in different forms, as he writes songs about God, songs to God, songs that encourage others to worship God, and also personal songs of worship written to God.

You may feel a pressure to write songs in a certain style at times, but none of us should box ourselves in and try to squeeze our songwriting into somebody else's mold. All we need to do is respond to God out of whatever He is revealing to us and out of our love for Him. Then, as we spend time in His presence, the songs He is leading us to write will flow naturally.

In short, be confident in your writing style. Over the years I have realized that I have to simply write what I write, not feeling a pressure to deliver the type of songs that others are writing. Of course we need to pursue growing in the skill of songwriting and learn from those more experienced songwriters around us. But usually most of us are writing out of what God is doing in *our* lives and in *our* churches, so what we write will naturally be different from what others are writing. Your journey is different from others', and you have been created uniquely. Feel free to let these things come out in your writing. Your church needs *your* songs, whether they are for congregational use or for personal worship. Both types of songs are valuable to God and to the church.

Now that we have fixed our eyes on Jesus and taken the pressure off ourselves, let's look at some practical things that are helpful to bear in mind when writing songs.

Read the Word

I was at a retreat for worship leaders, and fellow speaker Matt Redman was asked for suggestions on how to remain inspired and keep songwriting fresh. Matt said that the flow of his writing has a direct correlation to whether he is reading the Bible or not. When he is immersed in God's Word, the songs flow, but when he has not been spending as much time reading Scripture, the songs don't flow as freely.

Worship is a response to who God is and what He has done, so it makes total sense that reading the Bible would be the thing that inspires us to write songs. When we read His Word, the Holy Spirit reveals truth to us. He reveals more of who He is, and as we read, we learn about what God has done and about His incredible love for us. Let's get into the Word so we can know more of our God, become transformed by truth, and respond to Him in worship!

Theme

When it comes to God, there is so much to write about, such as His grace, His mercy, His love, the hope He brings, God the Father, Jesus, the Holy Spirit, God our healer, His strength, His splendor, His power, His majesty ... the list goes on and on. As we write, whether the songs are congregational or not, we need to ask ourselves what we are teaching the church through the lyrics of our songs.

Have you ever walked away from a church service unable to remember the bulk of the sermon? I know I have! But where we may struggle to remember the sermon, many of us often find ourselves singing a song we just sang in worship. Week in and week out we are singing worship songs over and over again, and so the words we sing will naturally enter our hearts and minds. That means there's quite a responsibility on our shoulders to communicate truth through our songs and to teach our congregations about all of who God is. If we are only writing songs about God the Father and Jesus but not about the Holy Spirit or about God's love and being near to Jesus but never about His majesty and power, our churches will probably walk away knowing only part of who God is. As God reveals Himself to us, we need to write songs that reflect all of who He is.

Ask the Holy Spirit to reveal more of who God is to you as you read His Word and spend time in His presence. And go on asking. He desires for us to know Him, and He will surely respond to your request.

Be creative

It can be easy to get stuck in a rut and use the same lyrics and chords when songwriting. Finding fresh ways to communicate a truth can be challenging, and it often takes time and effort to find that lyric you are looking for or to have a fresh musical idea. But there are tools to help us. Here are some suggestions:

- Read different versions of the Bible. There are many different versions of the Bible that communicate the same truth using different wording. There are so many great versions out there, such as the New International Version, the New Living Translation, the English Standard Version, The Message, the New King James Version, and many more. I have found BibleGateway.com a great resource when wanting to read a chapter or verse from different versions. You can search for the passage you want to read and click on the version you want to read it from—it's easy to navigate and really helpful.

- Use a thesaurus. Sometimes we need a little help to say something in a fresh way, and a thesaurus could be just the thing to help.

- Try a rhyming dictionary. Sometimes it can be hard to find a lyric that will work well thematically and within the section of a song you are working on. A rhyming dictionary will give you some ideas of words that rhyme with others in the section you are working on and may just be the tool that helps you complete it.

- Check out the Amplified Bible. Have you ever found it hard to fully understand what a Bible passage is saying? The Amplified Bible is a translation that helps explain the meaning of key words or phrases by giving alternatives, much like a thesaurus does, and by conveniently placing them in brackets right beside the text. It gives you an appreciation of how the original language was used, and I have found it a great tool for songwriting because it helps me explore different Bible themes and passages.

- Read and research. I have often found that the songs with strong lyrics and a firm theological foundation have been written by songwriters who research and read a lot about the themes they are writing about. The more that pours into us, the more there is to pour out. So it is incredibly valuable to be constantly reading and learning more about God.

- Learn some new chords. It can be really helpful to learn some new chords, even if it's just different ways to play a chord you already know. The slight variations can change the way a chord sounds, and that might spark something fresh.

- Write in different keys. Experimenting with writing songs in different keys can inspire fresh ideas for melodies and will push you to use different chords.

- Use another instrument. Playing a different instrument can inspire new musical and melodic ideas. For example, if your main instrument is a guitar, get a piano chord book, learn some chords, and try songwriting using a piano or keyboard. If you need help, find someone who plays a different instrument from you and write with that person. I have found this so helpful.

- Work with others. If you've been working on a song and you feel stuck, it can be really helpful to get together with another songwriter (we'll look at cowriting a bit later in this chapter), or some other musicians, and work on the song together. A fresh perspective is always helpful, and the different musical and melodic ideas that others can bring can be incredibly valuable when songwriting.

Record everything

There is nothing more frustrating than coming up with melodies or lyrics and then forgetting them, so it's really helpful to find some way to record all of your song ideas.

I have a Mac and use a program called GarageBand to record ideas. It's easy to use, and you get a clear recording. I also have a voice-recorder application for my phone, which is especially useful if I am away from my computer. These are just examples of what I use, but you can use any voice recorder to help record your ideas. Songs often evolve over time, and having ideas recorded enables you to go back to them for later use.

I recently heard a song written by a friend that I recognized from years ago—it had totally different verses and a modified chorus from when I first heard it. He had finally finished it years later, and now it's a great song. Proof that you should record everything! You never know when that idea you came up with will finally come together.

Keep going

I've found that songwriting comes in seasons. Sometimes it seems as though the songs just pour out, and at other times you can't come up with a fresh melody no matter how hard you try. Inventor Thomas Edison said that "success is 10 percent inspiration and 90 percent perspiration," and many songwriters have found this to be true.

It can often feel like a hard slog and can be quite frustrating at times. But keep going! Don't be discouraged. As you spend time with God, you will naturally respond with songs of worship to Him. Don't worry if not everything you write is amazing. Every songwriter you know of will have written songs you'll never hear because they weren't very strong ideas. So just keep going for it. The more you write, the more you will learn and grow in the skill of songwriting.

Get feedback

It's really helpful to let others hear your songs and receive feedback from them. Sometimes it's hard to see the changes needed when you have been working on a song for a while, and a fresh view can help to make the song better. Even so, one piece of advice I want to pass on is this: When I want to get feedback from those who will give constructive criticism, I make sure I choose people I trust and know are "for" me. Sharing your songs is such a vulnerable thing, and the whole process is more successful and will not be discouraging if you know and trust the person giving the criticism.

Once you receive feedback, you don't necessarily need to respond immediately. Often the people listening to the song as outsiders can see things you can't, and it can be hard to take their advice on an idea you have your heart set on when they feel it could be stronger. Get away and sit on it for a bit. I often find that their constructive criticism is right, and I end up reworking that section. Try not to be defensive, and remain open when you receive feedback from trusted others. If they are for you, they are only trying to help!

Make the call

As I mentioned previously, often the constructive criticism I receive has weight to it. But there are also times when after much thought

I don't agree with a suggestion. At times this has created a battle within me—take the advice or go with what I think is best?—and it's especially hard if my reviewer has been writing for longer than I have. But at the end of the day, I have learned that you have to go with your gut.

There have been times I have found it hard to know what choice to make, especially when a man is giving me feedback and it seems as though his suggestions are about a style or about lyrics he doesn't particularly connect with. I am in no way saying that we shouldn't listen to the feedback men give us, because in all honesty a lot of the time the men around me are spot-on! They bring such great wisdom. But as a female you're probably going to write in a style and use lyrics that women are more likely to connect with.

A few years ago I wrote a song called "Wash Me." When I played the song to another worship leader to get feedback, he said the lyrics "I long to run into Your arms" made him think of a woman in a white flowing dress running through a field. It totally made me laugh when he told me that, especially since I had written that song with the story of the Prodigal Son from Luke 15 in mind. I had no idea how he got the imagery of a woman in a flowing dress in his head. So funny! I later asked some other friends, including some women, for their opinions, and they said they thought the lyrics worked. I ended up sticking with what I originally wrote, realizing that these lyrics just didn't connect with that particular worship leader.

I encourage you to get feedback from both men and women. Try not to change the style or lyrics to something that doesn't fit with either your personality or your sex—the church needs the unique songs written by both men and women and will be blessed by them.

Personal or congregational?

There is so much freedom when writing personal worship songs— church musicians don't need to be able to play it, and congregations don't have to sing it. You have complete creative freedom and are able to share your personal journey with God and worship Him through song, much like King David did. These songs are so valuable to the church! They don't have to stay within the walls of your private room—though some may. Many times I have heard the words and melody of a song about a believer's personal walk with God, and I have connected with every word. These songs have helped me express my heart to God as I seek Him and worship Him privately. Although I may not use these songs when I lead worship, I am still grateful for them and see their value.

Songs written for corporate church worship are also incredibly valuable, because they enable us as a whole church to respond vocally to our God in worship. However, the freedom that we have when writing personal songs of worship is somewhat reduced when writing congregational worship songs. It's as though we need to put the lyrics and music through a filter in order to make the songs accessible to the congregation and enable them to easily engage with God.

Kathryn Scott is now going to share from her experience as a songwriter and give some guidelines for writing congregational songs.

Writing congregational songs
KATHRYN SCOTT

When we are writing for a whole congregation of people, there are some pretty special challenges we have to wrestle through. Our role as writers in this context is to give voice to everyone who will sing our song, as though it was their very own song to God. To do that effectively, we need to have some very clear goals; otherwise, our song will only ever express our heart and will not allow the church the opportunity to sing her own response to God.

Because worship is such a transparent, wonderfully relational, deeply spiritual thing, I want to encourage you to always start the writing process from where you are. Write from a depth of relationship with God. Spend yourself on Him. Learn to love Him in the normal stuff of life. Give Him your attention with your thoughts, and think of Him when you interact with the world around you. Find out what your own "language" is in expressing that. If you love solitude, take time out to be with Him. If you love to read, read. If you walk and love to be closer to Him in nature, try to find the time to do that. If you are up to your eyes in being a mother, love Him thoroughly by giving your all to your kids. This "language" sounds different for each one of us and will vary at every stage of life.

Write for your own congregation or small group

Don't try to write for the whole world. When we write for our own church, we get to look at the specific troubles and triumphs we are facing together—the things the Holy Spirit is stirring among us and leading us into—and we give our congregations the chance to express corporately the things we are journeying through together at that time.

If it turns out that such a song captures the heart of more than one church, then that's wonderful, but I don't think it's the starting place for a song. In fact, every time we finish a song, what happens with it next is entirely up to the Lord. He has taken songs that I thought were pretty mediocre and turned them into epics, and He has sometimes hidden songs that I thought were masterpieces. It just shows you how much I know about what makes a good song!

What I do know is that He has asked me to write, and if He has asked the same of you, the success is in the obedience: to write, and to learn to write, as well as you can. The rest is up to Him. He will determine the results.

When we write congregationally, we have this unbelievable opportunity to "fill in the gaps" in people's understanding of God (their theology). We can be listening to sermons or parts of teachings we've heard and taking the truth that's there, making them into songs that will feed people's souls and giving them words through which to offer their own response to the Father. Wow! I will never get tired of doing that!

Listen for the prophetic

There is something in catching the "wind" of what the Holy Spirit is doing in a season and crafting it into a song. Those songs simply ignite in people's hearts. Sometimes this is as simple as writing about what you feel is going on, as a theme among you congregationally. At other times the Lord will speak to you directly, or through someone else, and you will know. Write into those things.

Crafting a song

What about some of the practical elements of taking those initial "what am I going to write about" thoughts and turning them into songs that a whole body of people can sing with all their hearts? How do we craft the song? Aside from actually leading worship, this is one of my all-time favorite things.

Basically, the craft of writing for congregations is a pretty simple science, but it takes all of our ingenuity and creativity to put it into practice. When we are writing for everyone in a group of people to sing at once, the songs have to be easy to sing, full of truth, easy to understand, easy for a worship leader to lead, and easy to remember. To make this work, we need to give our attention to two main aspects:

- Melody. Our melodies must be "hooky." They have to be simple enough for everyone to sing. They can't be too tricky or have too much of a range within them; otherwise, only the very best singers will be able to pull them off, and congregations will just watch when they're sung. That's the opposite of what we're trying to do. I always encourage worship leaders to sing within the range from G below middle C up to D just over an octave above middle C. More people will be able to sing the song if you keep this in mind. Don't forget that you can arrange the song in a different key after it's written or use key changes and all sorts of wonderful things—but the song itself needs to be accessible for lots of people to be able to sing it. Arranging is not the same as writing.

- Lyrics. Our lyrics need to be well crafted. We only get one chance in a song to say exactly what we mean and to say it in a way that others will long to use as their very own words to God in worship. That takes time and patience. It means we have to embrace the art of rewriting.

I have a couple of really good friends who listen to what I've written and then give me constructive criticism. I can't tell you how helpful it is to have my songs heard by fresh ears. They'll often tell me that a line I've loved from the start of the writing process simply doesn't make sense. Or that I need to rethink the way I've put something across—maybe it's a little ambiguous or unclear. Sometimes they'll encourage me to dig deeper, to look for that better way of saying something, to push for the great rather than settle for the good. That sort of input is priceless.

Try it out

The final stage in the process is to try it out on the congregation. A song will take a couple of times through before you can tell if it has legs and is going to catch on. I usually introduce a song in church by trying it for a few weeks in a row. By about the third time, I know whether or not this is a song the church can worship with.

Finally, listen to the feedback of a select few (including your pastor)—and if they think it's a good song, then keep using it. If they really don't think there's mileage in it, don't be afraid to either rework it or retire it. Never be tempted to think the most recent song you've written is the last song you'll ever write. God is completely abundant. He is utterly inexhaustible in His creativity. And He is a lavishly generous Father. All of those things tell me that He has a whole lot more songs for you to write yet!

Beth Redman is now going to share from her experience in cowriting. Beth and her husband, Matt, have four children. An author and songwriter in her own right, she has cowritten songs such as "Blessed Be Your Name" and "You Never Let Go."

Cowriting
BETH REDMAN

God loves a team

There aren't too many things in the Christian life that are designed to be done on our own, lone-ranger-style. The more I've been involved in writing worship songs, the more I'm convinced that this is true for this ministry also. I'm not saying we should never write a song alone, but just that sometimes we can underestimate the skills, insight, and creativity we can draw upon by inviting a fellow songwriter into the mix. The simple fact is that God loves a team.

I've had the blessing of cowriting quite a few songs over the years. I love the fact that when you finish a song with a fellow writer, you know there was no way you would have arrived at that place without working with each other. Even the times when you don't end up with a finished song, you've probably still encouraged each other as Christians, had a Bible study together, and at the same time, sharpened each other's songwriting skills.

In the past few years most of the songs I've worked on have been with my husband, Matt. Whether we're working just on melodies together, or whether it's whole sections of songs, the key is honesty. You have to be willing to be honest and transparent; but find a humble and kind way to do that, because most people become quite sensitive in the songwriting process. If you don't express honest opinions, then you won't get anywhere very quickly.

On the other hand, if you are brutal or unkind in the way you share your thoughts, your approach can be destructive—not just to the songs, but to your fellow songwriter, too. Being harsh and shooting down every idea your cowriter has will create an environment where people will not feel free or confident to share new ideas. Creating a writing culture of honesty and kindness not only honors God but also makes for a much more creative environment. If you know the person you're writing with really well, as Matt and I do, you need to be especially careful not to be harsh. You need to honor each other's feelings and make comments or suggestions kindly and wisely.

As well as being honest, we also need to be flexible. Now and again you'll have to die to an idea or the way you want it done, because cowriting is a team process. No one gets to have his or her own way in every decision. Yes, you'll need to speak up (gently, humbly, and kindly) for the ideas and suggestions you feel strongly about, but you'll also need to give way sometimes on various ideas and suggestions when they are precious to your cowriter or cowriters. Cowriting always involves compromise, but the benefits of this far outweigh the costs.

At the end of the day, we are all creative types, sharing our thoughts, ideas, and feelings—things that are usually quite precious to us. As my husband says, "Bluntly telling someone their song is not very good is like telling someone their baby is not very good-looking—it's a big no-no!"

There is such strength in working as a team. When Matt and I wrote the song "You Never Let Go" together, it came out of a season of deep pain. I had experienced several miscarriages, and the future in that area looked very bleak. The song became a big statement of faith and trust for us, and in fact, we first sang it as a testimony to God's work in our lives at my thirtieth birthday party, which was full of friends, family, and neighbors, many of whom were not Christians. It was a powerful moment, but we both knew the song still needed some work to prepare it for congregational use.

We also knew that the song we had produced would never have reached the point it had if either one of us had been working alone. It was a matter of stretching each other to keep digging for the very best ideas and solutions for each line of the song. You can imagine that, with the sensitive nature of the lyrics and the pain of the miscarriages still very real, we had to be especially careful and considerate of each other's feelings.

When we write alone, we can sometimes be tempted to think, *That will do,* and settle on an idea, when actually there is still more work to be done if the song is to fulfill its maximum potential. You can help each other persevere, bouncing ideas around until you both feel pleased with the end result.

One last great thing about cowriting: The songwriting time is more likely to be put in your schedule and stay there. We all live busy lives, and when left on our own, songwriting can often take a backseat. Something else more pressing can so easily come up, and we miss out on the time we had originally scheduled to write. But cowriting has a different dynamic; we have made a commitment to someone else, and so we are much less likely to cancel the plans.

When it comes to songwriting, God loves a team!

To close this chapter on songwriting, Christy Nockels is going to share from her journey as a writer.

The everyday glorious
CHRISTY NOCKELS

I've been writing songs since I was a little girl. From the time I first learned to spell, I have been crafting small offerings of song from my heart. It started in the driveway of my family's home, looking out at God's creation; in fact, I still have some of those papers with scribbles and poems—evidence of a little mind for God even then.

Throughout college and the first few years of marriage, I could spend countless hours searching Scripture and studying melodies and lyrics of the great songwriters of past and present. I had no idea then what a luxury it was to have such a large capacity for all things poetic, melodic, and majestic. I'm constantly telling my songwriter friends who are single to soak up this time and take advantage of the opportunity to delve into writing while time is abundant.

Several years and three children later, my ability to retain any kind of information whatsoever has become challenged. (I really am at a place of being okay with it, I promise! In fact, I think it's rather comical at times.) My kids are precious, and they bring me a great deal of joy, but their little voices entering my psyche at every turn can sometimes overload my brain! Life is full at all times, and there's never a dull moment. I'm needed for homework help, laundry folding, bill paying, book reading, and of course, feeding my family. Then there are the emails and the phone calls, the ministry and the travel—it all means "hello" to what it takes to make life work for us and "good-bye" to songwriting by candlelight, if you know what I mean.

Because life has changed for me so much through the years, I've been through seasons where it has been very difficult for me to get any traction as a songwriter from day to day. I know now that this is because I felt the time I did have to offer God was not enough— nowhere near as much as it used to be. Because songwriting earlier in life was this amazing experience, I felt like the act of scheduling time to write was a disgrace.

I was meeting one day with an amazing woman I know and asked her with a lump in my throat, "How can I possibly write songs in the midst of everything I have going on in my life?" A very wise mother of nine children and a songwriter herself, she said, "You can invite the glorious into the everyday things." That one hit me hard, because now there was no excuse. Could it be true? The glorious could enter into my everyday, earthly stuff and bring melodies and songs of praise to God?

I was both relieved and terrified at the same time. I was relieved that there is a rhyme and reason to everything I do and that God is in every small detail of my day. The voices of my children swirling about me can silence the enemy, and waiting in traffic can become a birthplace for a song of hope. All things truly are held together by Him! Yet I was terrified that now there was no more hiding behind the stuff of life, the mundane, and all I had to accomplish each day.

The Lord has been gracious to show me that scheduling time to write songs is an act of obedience, because it's part of what He has called me to do. When you've invited Him into your everyday chaos, the moments that you do schedule time to sit before Him and write are much more productive and fruitful because you've been in step with Him all day. Even if it is only five minutes each day, or even if the song sounds awful to someone else, you've still had the courage to mimic your Creator in the way He fashioned you.

I keep a journal nearby at all times with thoughts and phrases in it, sometimes Scriptures or things that have pulled on my heart that day. I keep a digital voice recorder with me everywhere I go; otherwise, I might lose the melodies forever! And because of this, I have pieces of songs, moments from days gone by, that become something glorious ... eventually. As I bring those fragments into a carved-out space for writing, I'm reminded that God has been with me all the way. After all, He knows and understands my capacity, and He surprises me more and more with what I'm capable of if I commit myself fully to Him.

Even though life is much busier now, I'm thankful after all these years that I still have a longing to sing a new song every day to the Lord. I'm grateful that there's evidence at the end of the day, on a page full of scribbles and poems, that I still have a mind for Him and feel compelled to write about it!

9

The worship pastor

When I was one of the worship pastors for a church in the UK a few years ago, one of my responsibilities was to do all the administration for the worship team. This included organizing the worship rosters and team meetings. However, even though I felt that I was getting information out to the team clearly, some people were not reading the letters I sent them with key information about band practice and team meetings. Team members were either turning up late or not turning up at all. It was really frustrating.

Not knowing what to do, I sought God for guidance, and He led me to John 10:3–5, where Jesus says, "He calls his own sheep by name and leads them out. When he has brought out all his own, he goes ahead of them, and his sheep follow him because they know his voice. But they will never follow a stranger; in fact, they will run away from him because they do not recognize a stranger's voice." Verses 14–15 continue, "I am the good shepherd; I know my sheep and my sheep know me—just as the Father knows me and I know the Father—and I lay down my life for the sheep." As I read these verses, I realized that, although I had been running a tight ship when it came to administration, I wasn't being a very good shepherd to those on the team, and they weren't following me. So I began to ask God to reveal His heart for those on the team, and as He did, He gently began to show me *His* way of pastoring a worship team.

God has taught me so much over the past few years, both through observing others I have had the privilege of working with and through the sometimes painful business of making my own mistakes. I want to share with you some of the things I have learned from being part of a worship team—as a backing vocalist and worship pastor. And, most important of all, I want to share what we all can learn from the perfect biblical model for a pastor: Jesus.

Love and know your team members

One thing that truly stands out in Jesus as a leader is that He loved His disciples. He knew them and they knew Him. He didn't just tell them how to live their lives but showed them by example. He took care of them, fed them, shared meals with them, and taught them. He not only talked about how the Good Shepherd lays down His life for His sheep, but He also told the story of the lost sheep (Luke 15:4)—how the shepherd loves each individual sheep so much that he would leave all the others to find the one that was lost. Jesus teaches us through His Word and through His death on the cross that to love others means in some way to lay down our own lives for them.

Investing in the individual

Probably the biggest thing I have learned is that we need to love and value each individual member of the team. We have to take time to get to know them. This can be easy at times and more difficult at other times, depending on how well we naturally get along with different members of the team. But it is really important to make an effort with *every* team member. Inviting them to be part of the team requires commitment from them to pursue integrity, practice their instrument, serve the team, and to be at band practice on time, among other things. On the other hand, it also requires commitment from us as their worship pastors to invest in them in a number of ways, one of which is by building relationships with them.

I am not saying that we all have to become best buddies, and obviously when it comes to the opposite sex, it doesn't mean hanging out one-on-one all the time, but you can still make those members of the worship team feel valued. For example, you could encourage them after they play, sing, or do sound on a Sunday. Or you could gather a couple of your team members and meet up for lunch or coffee. Ask God to give you a heart for each person—to see them through His eyes and to know more of His love for them. Spend time praying for them. As God reveals His heart for them, you will naturally find yourself caring about them more and will be active in building relationships with them.

I have learned that if we are only communicating with the team when we want them to play, they won't feel valued. If they don't feel valued, they won't feel safe. By "safe" I mean accepted, loved for who they are, and free to be creative. If they don't feel safe, they won't listen to us. Like the sheep that don't follow the stranger, if they don't

know us, they won't follow us. This doesn't mean we have to share
our deepest thoughts and fears with them, but, just as Jesus let His
disciples know Him, we must let our team members know us. If they
feel they know us, they will trust us.

Investing in the team

In the Bible we find many examples of Jesus hanging out with His
disciples. He spent loads of time with them and ate with them fre-
quently. Although it was different then, in that Jesus traveled and
lived with the disciples for three years, we can still learn from His
example. Our worship team has found it really helpful to gather
together regularly and eat a meal or just hang out. It's been so important in building a sense of team because it gives everyone a chance to
get to know each other away from their instruments. This has such
a positive impact when we play together on Sundays and helps us to
gel together as a band. Loving and knowing the individual will mean
that when we notice strengths and weaknesses in that person, we will
encourage or challenge him or her with a heart of love.

Encouragement

We all need encouragement. In 1 Thessalonians 5:11, we are told to
"encourage one another and build each other up." Creative people
are often quite sensitive. As musicians, we often wear our hearts on
our sleeves when we play or sing. I know I often walk away from
a time of leading worship feeling completely raw and vulnerable.
So encouraging the team members is crucial. We need to encourage

them if they play a cool guitar riff—or when they show up on time! I know you might think, *Well, they should turn up on time anyway—why do I have to thank them?* But I guarantee that, if we acknowledge the things they do well, they will be more likely to receive constructive criticism and not miss the positive things we say. And they will be more likely to practice and be creative, or show up on time regularly, if they have been encouraged and feel appreciated.

We also have to remember to encourage them in things that aren't dependent on their skills. All of us long to be encouraged in who we are, not just what we do, so we should remember to treat the team members in the way we would want to be treated. Worship team members often end up serving week in, week out; and although this is an incredible privilege, even the most dedicated people need to know they are valued.

Saying the hard stuff

Probably one of the hardest realities of pastoring a worship team is saying the hard stuff. No one likes to be the bearer of bad news, or even the slightly not nice news. But the truth is that, if we truly love the individual, we will want the best for him or her. If we never mention the stuff we see that needs to be challenged, they will never be able to grow. Hebrews 12:11 says, "No discipline seems pleasant at the time, but painful. Later on, however, it produces a harvest of righteousness and peace for those who have been trained by it." As kindly as you can try to say it, telling people they need singing lessons is never going to be great fun; neither is challenging someone who has become tainted by pride, or even speaking to someone about having a break from up-front ministry because their private life isn't matching up to the public one. But if we see these things in members of our team and we love them, we have to say it. We have to communicate. We can't allow team members to find they are playing or singing less and less when they don't know why.

Always remember that every individual situation is different. Everyone has a different past and their own insecurities, so we have to ask the Holy Spirit for the best way to deal with each situation. For one person certain action might be necessary, when for another it could be inappropriate. We have to use discernment.

We all need to be challenged at times in order to grow, so it's important that, alongside encouraging our team members in who they are, we challenge them to grow in their skills. It is biblical to strive for excellence in our skills as members of the worship team. Psalm 33:3 says, "Sing to him a new song; play skillfully, and shout for joy." It's important to encourage musicians and singers to invest in gear that will help their playing or to attend the lessons that would develop their abilities. We need to encourage them to be practicing their skills, to be working on them, and to be learning the songs well. This will make their confidence grow and will be a blessing to the worship team and the congregation.

We can always grow and learn more. A few years ago one of the worship leaders I was working with told me he was going to take more vocal lessons when he moved to his new job. He has an amazing voice, so I was thinking, *How good do you want your voice to be?* But he simply said he wanted to stretch himself. That's a great example, because it would have been easy for him to sit happily where he was, but out of humility he chose to pursue growing in skill.

So how do you say the hard stuff?

My husband, Paul, and I talk these things through because we work together to pastor our worship team, but we also consult the leader of our church at times. We may ask him for guidance and wisdom over how to deal with a situation because he has more pastoral experience.

It's important to find the right timing to say the hard stuff. For example, it's probably not very sensitive to speak to someone about needing singing lessons just before they go up to sing or just after they have been singing. Wait for the right time when that person will not feel exposed and will be able to go away and process what you have spoken to them about in private. I have found that when you know the members of your team and meet up with them regularly, it's a lot easier to find a place to bring these things up. Relationship is key!

We have also found it can be really helpful to pull other leaders in the church into these situations. For example, if the person you need to meet with is in a small group, you could invite their small group leader to be there when you meet with them. This is a great way to make sure that they will be supported and encouraged while you discuss your concerns with them.

Feed them

Practical training

It's also important to feed the members of our worship team in practical areas. Your church could invest in group vocal lessons for the backing vocalists and worship leaders or invest in training for the sound technicians. It makes such a difference in the confidence and ability of those on the team, and it encourages them to pursue getting better at their skills outside of church practice times.

Worshipping together

Worship team members are often leading, playing, or singing during the church service, so it is really valuable to create space where they can worship together outside of those services. At our church we meet once a month to worship together. We put out a few guitars, a keyboard, some percussion, and we just lead one another in worship. It gives us space to be creative and to worship without the responsibility of leading the congregation.

At our previous church, my husband introduced to the worship team something called Dancing in the Dark. We would turn out the lights, crank up worship music, and everyone would spread out across the building and dance or respond to God in whatever way they wanted to. Some people shouted, some jumped, some even ran around. It was a really fun yet intimate time with God. When we did it as a team, the response was amazing. People loved worshipping God away from their instruments, and everyone said they felt such freedom. It was amazing to observe many team members who had never responded to God through dance now feel the freedom to do so. The music is loud, the lights are low, and it's a great, unintimidating way for the team to just go for it and worship God. Give it a go—it's so fun!

Prayer

We have also found it valuable to create space when others in the church pray for the worship team—a time when the team can simply receive and be refreshed and inspired. When you are playing during the services at church, you don't always get the chance to receive prayer, so this is a wonderful time to receive from God.

Look to Jesus

When it comes to being a pastor, Jesus set the best example. The disciples learned from watching Him, listening to Him, and asking Him questions. He taught them how to "feed His sheep" by the way He loved them. He taught them how to heal people by doing it first. He taught them how to treat people as they watched Him treat others with incredible love and compassion. He taught them the cost of following Him by paying the greatest cost on the cross.

It's vitally important that we are following Jesus, so that those who follow us will also follow Him. We must remember that …

- If we want the team to be at worship practice on time, we need to be.

- If we want to teach the team to value people, we must value people.

- If we want the team to be humble, we must pursue humility.

- If we want to teach people to serve, we must first serve them.

- If we want to teach people to embrace constructive criticism, we need to do so as well.

- If we want the team to pursue musical excellence, so must we.

- If we want people to pursue their personal relationships with Jesus, we must always be in pursuit of Him.

I have learned more about the person I want to be and have been inspired to change by observing others who love people and make them feel valued. The team is going to learn from our example as leaders, good or bad. It is a total privilege to lead a worship team, so let's pour ourselves out to help our team members thrive and become all they are called to be.

Practical responsibilities of a worship pastor

Recruiting new musicians

One of the main responsibilities of a worship pastor is to recruit new musicians into the worship team. For some this may seem like a straightforward task—if they can play music, they're in! However, being a musician or singer on a worship team is not just a servant role, it's also a leadership role. The worship team members are usually in a prominent place in the church; not only are they setting an example to others, but they are also representing the values of your church. So it's crucial that you bring musicians into the team who are musical *and* who uphold the values of your church and set an example that you would encourage others to follow. As a worship pastor, it's important to know who is being put in that leadership role—for everyone's sake: the individual's, the worship team's, and the church's. To help you recruit musicians who will be a blessing to your worship team and your church, I would like to share with you important qualities to look for in a candidate.

But first ...

Get to know them!

Many musicians move to a new church enthusiastic about getting involved in the worship team, and they are likely to approach you, the worship pastor, and let you know they are interested in joining. It can be tempting to let them start playing up front immediately, particularly if they are great musicians or if you really need their specific instruments in your band. However, it is my advice that you let them be part of the church for four to six months before they get involved. This is something that my husband and I have found to be wise, and it's a boundary we put in place for four reasons.

First, it gives us a chance to get to know them; we aren't going to be able to answer any of the other questions we may have if we haven't spent any time with them and gotten to know them.

Second, it gives them a period of time when they can attend church with no responsibilities. Musicians are often burned out from being involved in church services week in, week out; so when someone begins attending our church, we want to bless them and give them time and space to rest and become refilled spiritually.

Third, in my experience some musicians move to a new church with wounds they carry from their time on other worship teams. So this brief stretch of downtime is a great opportunity for them to receive healing and freedom. If they were to jump straight back into up-front ministry, those wounds may not have proper time to heal. It is better for them and for the team if they begin the journey of healing before joining.

Finally, this time period also enables us to see whether they are committed to the church. Are they involved in the church in other ways? Are they part of a small group? Do they attend church regularly? Do they attend churchwide events? It's important to have people on the worship team who are committed to and excited about the vision of the church.

Here are some other questions you may want to ask yourself as you search to find musicians and singers who will be a blessing to your worship team.

Are they true worshippers?

Along with the worship leader, the role of the worship team is to lead God's people into His presence, so it is vital that the people on the team are passionate worshippers. This passion is what you should look for first. It can be tempting to compromise your values to get people involved because of their musical skills, especially if you are lacking a musician in one particular area. But I believe it is better to, say, have no drummer at all, than to have a great drummer who is not passionate about Jesus and worshipping Him. You can often tell whether someone is a passionate worshipper by observing them at church. If they are keen to play in the band but during times of worship are consistently standing there, twiddling their thumbs, and not singing, I'd probably wonder whether they love to worship or whether they just love to play music. Mike Pilavachi puts it this way: "If they can worship at the back, they can worship at the front." If someone truly worships and engages with God when they are part of the congregation and out of the public eye, then they can probably be trusted in a position of leadership.

One of the worship leaders at my church is a perfect example of this. This guy *loves* the Lord and loves to worship Him. No matter where he is in the congregation, whether he is standing in the front row, on the balcony with the youth group, at the sound desk doing sound, or whether he's in a small-group setting like our staff worship times, this guy is always engaging with God. He serves whenever needed, never pushes himself forward, and is so kind. He is such a blessing to have on the team. He is a true worshipper.

Are they servants?

Using our gifts to worship God and serve the church is an incredible privilege. Being part of a band means remembering that you are there to give and to serve. Although it is often someone's dream and passion to be on the worship team, they still need to remember that they are involved first to serve—it's not about them.

When my husband and I moved houses after we were first married, one of the worship leaders at our church offered to drive a removal van to help us put some of our things in storage. He spent a whole Saturday with us just to help us out. And it wasn't only on that occasion—he was always giving of himself to help other people out, whether that was at church or during the rest of the week. His servant heart wasn't just switched on for Sundays. He was a great asset to that team and set an example for the rest of us to follow.

Are they humble?

Philippians 2:8 says, "Being found in appearance as a man, he humbled himself and became obedient to death—even death on a cross!" As Jesus humbled Himself, we too must humble ourselves. Many musicians have learned to play or sing in an environment where they were encouraged to perform and show off their skills. However, worship is not a performance or a place for any of us to draw attention to ourselves. This doesn't mean that those on your team can't play or sing to the best of their ability, or use their creativity, because skill and creativity are incredibly valuable and bring glory to God. But their hearts must be in pursuit of Jesus being lifted up and serving the congregation in leading them to Him.

Are they teachable?

It is so important to have a teachable heart. It is amazing to be on a team where the musicians want to grow and improve their skills. However, not all musicians are active in pursuing this. As a worship pastor you may have to encourage them to get lessons or to keep practicing, and this is why it is crucial that the people on the team are teachable. They need to be willing to receive any constructive criticism you give them and actively respond to it. If you say to someone,

"That guitar sound is great, but I'm not sure if it works well in this song. Would you be able to use a more clean sound?" the person with a teachable heart will receive what you have said, whether they agree or not, and will respond gladly to your request.

This applies when attitudes and behaviors need to be challenged too. If you feel someone's attitude conflicts with the values of your team, you may need to address the issue with that person. At these times, it's important to know that they will receive what you have said and will take it to heart.

How do they work with others?

As the cliché says, there's no *I* in *TEAM*, so it is really important that the band consists of people who are team players. It's a lot of fun and such a joy to serve in the band when everyone is "for" one another and encourages one another. It is not for us to be desperate to be heard. Instead we should desire to work together to create a beautiful, collective sound that honors God.

Some musicians have responded to this by saying, "Why can't I play the way I want to? This is how I express my worship to God!" But there is a difference between personal worship and leading congregational worship. When my husband, Paul, plays drums in his personal worship, he can do as many fills and complicated rhythms as he likes. During these times, as he is pouring out his heart to God, he has total freedom to play ridiculously loud if he wants to. But he plays very differently in congregational worship. It's not that he isn't creative, or that he doesn't go for it, but he recognizes that he is there to use his instrument to lead the congregation in worship and to complement what is being played around him, not to overpower the rest of the band. He is aware of what the bass player is doing, what the electric guitarist is playing, and he is listening to the worship leader. He is being a team player. Good team members will listen to what others are playing or singing and will be sensitive to this, not being a distraction to the congregation. They will know when to back off and when to play strongly.

So how in practice do you recruit new musicians?

Now that a potential new recruit has shown commitment to your church and has displayed the qualities we looked at previously, you will need to hear them play their instrument, sing, or mix sound.

Here are two options that I have seen work well: One option is to use the traditional auditioning process, where a potential new recruit will play or sing on their own in front of their worship pastor, and their musical ability will be assessed in that environment. For many, this has proved to be really effective.

Another option is to hear the musicians play in a group setting. This is what we have chosen at our church, and we call it the Worship Jam. It is an evening at the church where any musicians interested in being part of the worship team, or who simply love to play music and want an opportunity to jam, can come and play in a nonthreatening band setting. We usually get a few of our regular team members to attend and go through a couple of songs in a specific arrangement, and then we interchange the musicians and singers and give them an opportunity to play with the others. This enables us to hear them play or sing and see how they work in a band setting.

Because it is a live setting, this is a great opportunity to hear someone mix sound as well. We have chosen to do the Worship Jam because it's a fun environment and it's a churchwide event that is not just for auditioning new worship team recruits. And so it minimizes the whole rejection aspect that straight auditioning can bring.

In the end, of course, each church is unique, so the way you choose to hear people play their instruments or sing is going to depend on how you feel it would best work at your church. There is no right or wrong way—just go with what works at your church.

New recruits

When you have decided to ask someone onto the team, one thing we have found really helpful is to create a Worship Team Values Form that each team member must read and sign before they commit to the team. This is in no way a binding contract. It's just a way for us to know that they understand their role and are onboard with the values of the team. It means that all of us are on the same page and that they know what the expectations are, avoiding any confusion down the road. The form also outlines our commitment to them: to serve, train, develop, and encourage them as best as we can.

In addition, we give each new worship team member a three-month trial. We put this in place so that both we and the new member can see whether the worship team is the right ministry for them to be involved in. Almost every time we all agree that it's the right place for them to serve. However, the three-month trial period has been really helpful in those rare circumstances when we have needed to reassess a person's involvement. Having this trial period simply gives new team members a heads-up that we are going to meet with them after three months, and at that time, we'll all have a time to voice any questions or concerns, as well as encouragement of course!

Administrative responsibilities

Many of the worship pastors I have come across are not exactly born administrators, and I include myself in this. As I mentioned earlier, I was a secretary for a year and learned a lot during that time, but administration is not my passion or my greatest skill. But as worship pastors a huge part of our role includes administration and organization. So let's look at some of the administrative aspects of leading a worship team.

Worship rosters

There are many different ways to organize the worship rosters for your team. Some worship pastors organize their rosters months in advance, some week by week, and others (such as myself) monthly. How you organize your worship rosters will often depend on the size of your worship team. If you have a large team, you will often have the freedom to have set bands or mix up the musicians if you want. However, if you are leading a smaller worship team, you may not have those options—you just have to work with what you've got.

Whatever size your team is, when organizing the worship rosters, you will first have to find out when your team members are available to play or sing. To obtain this information, at some point during the middle of the month I send out an email to the worship team members requesting their availability for next month. When I have received their replies, I create a document that includes the dates of the services for that month and space to insert the names of the worship leader, musicians, singers, and sound technicians for each service. This is an example of one week:

Sunday, July 18
   Worship Leader:
   Drums:
   Electric Guitar:
   Bass:
   Keys:
   Backing Vocals:
   Sound:

The first position I fill is the worship leader. When I am choosing who should lead on what date, I look at the roster from the previous month in order to know who led that month and how much. I also bear in mind what services are going to take place in the coming month. For example, if I were to organize the worship roster for March or April, I probably wouldn't put a new worship leader down to lead worship for the Easter service. Usually a lot happens during that service, and we often sing many hymns, which can be quite daunting for someone new to leading worship; so I would put one of the more experienced worship leaders down to lead for that service.

After I have placed the worship leaders onto the roster, I fill the rest of the positions, comparing both availability and musical skill. If possible, it's a great idea to put weaker musicians with stronger ones. For example, if you have a weaker bass player, put them down to play with a solid drummer. This will give the bass player more confidence and in turn will improve the overall sound. It will also put you at ease, knowing that there is one solid musician who will help keep the band together.

Get creative

One thing you are likely to experience at some point when organizing worship rosters is the sudden realization that you lack a particular kind of musician. At these times you need to get creative! The church I work for currently is a new church plant—we are only four years old. So there have been times when we have been lacking musicians and I've just had to mix it up. When we don't have a bass player, for example, I have often stripped the band down to just the worship leader, keys, percussion, and backing vocals. When we're missing an electric guitarist, the worship leader may choose to lead on electric guitar. We have found that the times we have had to change things up have actually brought great freshness and become amazing times of worship. It has reminded us that it's not about a formula and has pushed us to step out.

Changing up the band, then, is not only a necessity when you are lacking a certain musical instrument; it's also a good thing to try in order to keep things fresh. Whether you add more singers or another worship leader, use two electric guitarists instead of one, or totally strip down the band, changing it up is fun, and the result can sound great. We have found that it can encourage and challenge the congregation to step out of their comfort zone, where they are used to the band looking and sounding a certain way. Although you may often use a full band, don't feel like it has to be the same every week.

Training and equipping other worship leaders

One of the great privileges we have as leaders is the opportunity to invest in others. We get to pour out the knowledge and experience we have gained into the lives of others, in order to help them grow and thrive in the things they have been created to do. We don't have to be experts—most of the time others are just longing for someone to come alongside them, encourage them, and believe in them. Being that person is one of the most exciting rewards of being a worship pastor!

As worship pastors we have a responsibility to train and equip other worship leaders. We need to be asking God to show us the true worshippers, both the men and the women, whom He is calling to lead His people in worship. If you feel that God is prompting you to start investing in someone, spend time with that person (within safe boundaries if they are of the opposite sex of course), encourage them, and resource them in any way you can with the practical aspects of leading worship. Then at the right time, start giving them opportunities to lead. Be there when they lead if possible, so you can support them and give them feedback. And if they are successful and are growing in their gifts, be excited for them. Don't let jealousy enter your heart or respond out of insecurity. Remember that we are all unique and equally valuable, and we need to be onboard with what God is doing even when it may cause things to look different for us.

There is so much blessing when we fight for, not against, the things of His kingdom.

It's all about the local church!

Have you ever been to a major worship event and felt swept up in the joy and excitement that come when a huge gathering of believers meet together? I certainly have. Something special happens when believers from different churches and nations come together to worship God and hear His Word. I have been impacted by events like these; and in fact, I've had the privilege of leading worship at such events. It has been so much fun and so encouraging to know that people will leave inspired and equipped to serve their local churches.

As worship leaders and worship pastors, such events are bliss to us—everyone is there to worship, and everyone is "going for it." When we return to our local churches and are again faced with the challenge of leading our congregations and pastoring our worship teams, it can be easy to feel discouraged, and we can be tempted to hold those events on a pedestal. But let me encourage you: Even with all the excitement and powerful times of worship that are experienced at such events, the local church is where it's at! The local church is the main event.

As I write, Paul and I have been leading the worship team at our church for nearly three years, and I can honestly tell you that it has been one of the most rewarding things we've ever done. Yes, we've faced some huge challenges! We came from the UK, so our experience of church was quite different from the experience of those here in the US, particularly in the South. I was used to leading worship for youth and college students, whereas our church here in Florida is filled with believers of all ages, races, and socioeconomic backgrounds. Previously I had been used to leading in environments where people passionately expressed worship to God, but when we first moved here, many had come from church backgrounds where worship was not a focal part of the service. Even though they were hungry to worship God, many didn't know how to express their worship to Him. Much of our focus has had to be on encouraging our congregation to express their worship to God.

We came from a church that had a large pool of musicians, and when we moved to Florida, our worship team consisted of only a few. As a result, we have had to be really intentional about recruiting and training new musicians, both in the practical and spiritual aspects of leading worship. Thankfully God has provided the most amazing servant-hearted team members, and we are so grateful for them!

I really want to encourage you if you are leading worship and a worship team week in, week out—it takes time, but it's worth it! We are not all going to be at the same church from the day we become a Christian till the day we die—God moves us around for various reasons. But one thing I know to be true is that change and growth take time, and the only way to see God move in the lives of those around us is to be committed to them and to be patient. Paul and I have had the total privilege of seeing God transform the hearts and minds of those in our church and on our team in such a powerful way over the past year. It's been amazing to see. There were times in the previous years when we felt discouraged because the fruit we are seeing now did not seem so abundant then. However, we know now that God was moving powerfully all along and that it just took time for all that He was doing to break through to the surface.

There is so much joy to be found in committing to and serving your local church. We not only find love, support, and community, we also get to be that for others. And we get to experience the exciting journey of following Christ together, seeing His kingdom come and our communities transformed by His love and power!

10

Rise up & sing

When I was growing up, *The Little Mermaid* was one of my favorite movies. If you haven't seen it, it's about a mermaid named Ariel who has the most stunning voice. One day she swims to the surface of the ocean and sees a man, Prince Eric, on a ship and falls in love with him. Because he is human, she can't be with him, so she makes a deal with Ursula, the evil octopus, who gives her legs so she can walk on land and be with Prince Eric. The price of the deal is her voice. Ariel's gift is taken away from her, and she is left totally voiceless. There's more to the story, but my favorite scene is toward the end of the movie when King Triton, Ariel's father, defeats Ursula, and Ariel's voice is restored and she begins to sing.

Whenever I think about women rising up and leading worship, I am reminded of that scene. To me it's a picture of how the enemy has left so many women voiceless. There must be so many women out there whom God has called to lead but who have been discouraged and crushed and don't even believe they *can* lead. It's also a picture of how God, our Father, longs to restore a voice to the voiceless, so they can rise up and sing.

God has given each of us a song to sing with our lives, and as I mentioned earlier, for me that song is healing. My passion is to see people healed and set free and for their hope to be restored. It's something that God spoke to me about and confirmed through others years ago, before I ever led worship at church. The theme of healing will often be found when I am leading worship, and it runs through some of my songs. The song I have received the most positive feedback about is called "Heaven Rejoices." I wrote it in fifteen minutes. It's a word of encouragement and hope that I felt God gave me for a friend who was going through a really hard time. "Heaven Rejoices" is never going to win a Dove Award or be sung by thousands, but as it did for my friend, it has brought hope to some people who really needed to hear those words, and that is what I long for.

The song that God has placed on your heart to sing is going to be unique. Ask Him what it is. Listen to what stirs in your heart. Is your passion to see justice? Or is it to tell the world of His majesty and awesomeness? Whatever it is, go for it! Sing it out, write those songs! The Creator has created you to reflect who He is in a way that no one else can. Be bold. Find your confidence in Him. Remember that no matter what, the King loves you and delights in you, and He longs to see you, His daughter, be all that He created you to be. Cling to Christ, for …

> It's in Christ that we find out who we are and what we are living for. Long before we first heard of

Christ and got our hopes up, he had his eye on us,
had designs on us for glorious living, part of the
overall purpose he is working out in everything and
everyone.

—Ephesians 1:11–12 MSG

Thank you ...

Mum and Rob: Thank you so much for all you've done for me over the years, and for always believing in me and encouraging me.

Paul: You are the best husband ever. Thank you for loving me just the way I am. You've always cheered me on and supported me in the things I am passionate about, and I am so grateful. Thank you for your help with the book. I love that we get to work together for His glory. Go Team Buckley!

Si: Thank you for encouraging me to write this book. Paul and I value your friendship so much.

Les, Sally, Richard, and everyone at Kingsway: Thank you for believing in me and for everything you've done over the years. You guys are amazing!

Don, Sarah, Amy, Jack, and the team at David C. Cook: Thank you so much for publishing this book and for all the hard work you've done.

Liza: Thank you so much for all your hard work, support, encouragement, and friendship. I'm so grateful.

Ali, Pete, Beth C., Jodi, and Sally: Thanks so much for reading through the manuscript and giving your feedback. Your feedback has been so helpful.

Christy and Kathryn: What a joy and privilege to have you contribute to the book. Your hearts, wisdom, and experiences have brought so much, and I am so grateful.

Beth: Thank you so much for all your support and encouragement over the years—it has meant so much. It's been an honor to have you contribute to the book.

Andy: Thank you so much for your friendship. You are such a faithful friend, and I am so thankful for all the encouragement and support you have given me over the years, especially when I first started singing backing vocals and leading worship.

Tim: Thank you for getting me involved in leading worship. I've learned so much from you. You and Rach set an amazing example of passionate worshippers who honor God with their lives, and I'm so grateful that I have had the privilege of spending time with you guys and learning from you.

Matt: Thank you for the amazing example you have set for those of us who feel passionate about worship and leading God's people into His presence—one of purity of heart and humility. I'm just so grateful that I've had the opportunity to learn from you.

Fowler: Thank you for being an amazing boss and pastor. Thank you for believing in me, always supporting me, and releasing me into the things God has called me to.

Ed: Thank you for being such a great and faithful friend to our family. Paul and I love working with you, and we're so grateful for all you do.

River City Church staff: Thanks so much for cheering me on over the past year. You guys are amazing! I love working with you all.

River City Church: You are an amazing worshipping church. I love the journey God has taken us on over the past few years—it's been amazing to see all that He has done! Thanks so much for your encouragement; it means so much.

Mike P. and Soul Survivor: *Thank you* so much for believing in me and for the amazing opportunities I had to serve and worship with you. My love and passion for worship and the values instilled in me came from my time in the UK, and I am so, so grateful.

And most of all I want to thank Jesus for saving me, healing me, and giving me such amazing hope.

Glossary

Capo: A capo is a clamplike devise that when placed on the neck of a guitar shortens the strings and therefore raises the pitch of the instrument. It's used so that the guitarist can play open chords in keys that would usually require barre chords.

Chord charts: Chord charts are a way of notating music that outlines the basic harmonic and rhythmic form of a song.

Mic: Microphone.

Pads/Synth: Pads and synthesizers are played by the keys player and can take the form of a wide array of sounds. They are usually based on other instruments (such as strings, brass, choirs, etc.) and then tweaked with various effects to produce a very full sound.

Riff: A riff is a repeated chord progression, pattern, refrain, or melodic line played by the rhythm section or a solo instrument.

Stage monitor: A stage monitor is a speaker placed onstage that enables the musician to hear instruments and vocals when playing live. For example, a guitarist might have a stage monitor that has the lead vocal, keys, bass, and drums in it so that he or she can hear the rest of the band clearly.

Stage tuner: A stage tuner is often in the form of a guitar pedal that enables the guitarist to silently tune their guitar by muting the signal out when the pedal is in operation. The pedal displays the note being played and directs the guitarist to the correct pitch.

Bibliography

Bevere, Lisa. *Fight Like a Girl*. New York: Warner Faith/FaithWords, 2008.

Bible Gateway, www.biblegateway.com.

Buckley, Lex. "Heaven Rejoices," *Through the Valley* © 2006 Thankyou Music.

Christian Copyright Licensing International, www.ccli.com.

Hughes, Tim. "Everything," *Holding Nothing Back* © 2006 Thankyou Music.

Hughes, Tim. *Passion for Your Name*. Eastbourne, East Sussex, UK: Kingsway/David C. Cook, 2003.

Hughes, Tim, and Ben Cantelon. "Happy Day," *Holding Nothing Back* © 2006 Thankyou Music.

Kingsway, www.kingsway.co.uk.

The Lockman Foundation, www.lockman.org/amplified.

Morgan, Jeannie. *Let the Healing Begin.* Eastbourne, East Sussex, UK: Survivor/David C. Cook, 2007.

Redman, Matt. *The Heart of Worship Files.* Ventura, CA: Regal Books, 2003.

Redman, Matt. "Nothing but the Blood," *Facedown* © 2004 Thankyou Music.

Redman, Matt, and Beth Redman. "Blessed Be Your Name," *Where Angels Fear to Tread* © 2002 Thankyou Music.

MIRIAM WEBSTER
MADE ME GLAD

Available from iTunes